Real Estate in Italy

T0271093

This in-depth case study evaluates the recent evolution of the Italian real estate market, which has lately been subject to two interlocking phenomena: a serious devaluation of physical assets and, at the same time, a deep legislative innovation of the vehicles investing in this asset class.

The novelty of the legal framework of some of the Italian real estate investment vehicles and the recent developments in the market make this detailed analysis a fascinating addition to the literature.

The book starts with an analysis of the Italian real estate sector, covering the evolution and performance in light of the economic crisis and the most recent legislative innovations. Italian real estate investment vehicles are then compared with a broader European perspective. Each Italian investment vehicle (real estate investment funds, real estate fixed capital investment companies and real estate investment trusts) is then analysed in both legal and financial details, providing insights into management structure, the rights and powers of investors, the typical investment process and the related costs. The different management models are then compared in order to assess their advantages and disadvantages, especially for institutional investors. The performance measurement of Italian closed-end alternative investment funds and the phenomenon of discount to net asset value for listed real estate investment funds are then subject to a theoretical and empirical examination.

Guido Abate is Assistant Professor of Financial Markets and Institutions in the Department of Economics and Management at the University of Brescia, Italy. He holds an M.Sc. in finance from Bocconi University, Italy, and a Ph.D. in financial markets and institutions from the University of Bologna, Italy. He is the author of several international publications and his main fields of research are alternative asset classes, indexed investments and behavioural finance.

Giuditta Losa, MRICS, holds a B.Sc. in business administration, an M.Sc. in architecture and another Master's degree in real estate management. She has gained 20 years of experience in real estate as an asset manager in a public company, a fund advisor in the global firm CBRE and as Head of Real Estate Italy in a bank controlled by Commerzbank AG. She is currently Manager of Operations & Corporate Affairs in COIMA SGR.

International Real Estate Markets

The Chinese Real Estate Market
Development, Regulation and Investment
Junjian Cao

Real Estate in Italy
Markets, Investment Vehicles and Performance
Guido Abate and Giuditta Losa

Real Estate in Italy
Markets, Investment Vehicles and Performance

Guido Abate and Giuditta Losa

Routledge
Taylor & Francis Group

LONDON AND NEW YORK

First published 2017
by Routledge
2 Park Square, Milton Park, Abingdon, Oxon OX14 4RN

and by Routledge
711 Third Avenue, New York, NY 10017

Routledge is an imprint of the Taylor & Francis Group, an informa business

© 2017 Guido Abate and Giuditta Losa

British Library Cataloguing-in-Publication Data
A catalogue record for this book is available from the British Library

Library of Congress Cataloging in Publication Data
A catalog record for this book has been requested.

ISBN: 978-1-138-23151-1 (hbk)
ISBN: 978-1-315-31520-1 (ebk)

Typeset in Times New Roman
by Swales & Willis Ltd, Exeter, Devon, UK

Contents

Acknowledgements

The authors would like to express their gratitude to: Prof. Ignazio Basile (University of Brescia), Manfredi Catella (COIMA), Prof. Pierpaolo Ferrari (University of Brescia and SDA Bocconi School of Management), Davide Braghini (Gianni, Origoni, Grippo, Cappelli & Partners), Paola Fico (Borsa Italiana), Marco Frulio (Gianni, Origoni, Grippo, Cappelli & Partners), Gabriella Goglia (Agenzia delle Entrate), Biagio Izzo (Maisto e Associati), Giacomo Morri (SDA Bocconi School of Management), Kelly Russell (COIMA), Sergio Sinisi (Banca d'Italia) and Marco Valdonio (Maisto e Associati).

Foreword

The book provides an analysis of the Italian property and financial real estate sectors in the context of the legislative innovations recently introduced as part of the structural reforms approved by the government.

The current legislation for real estate investments in Italy favours the development of a transparent real estate sector in line with best international market practices, facilitating the entrance of international capitals.

This analysis will be useful for investors, providing them with the main characteristics of real estate investment vehicles in Italy, with a comparison to similar vehicles in other EU countries.

The Italian government has updated the current regulatory regime in compliance with European Union Directives, reinforcing existing investment products and introducing new forms of real estate investment vehicles.

The study also covers the impact of the EU directive AIFMD on Italian financial real estate.

Despite an increase of compliance controls, the new directives and rules will make it easier for alternative investment managers to build more efficient, scalable and recognisable pan-European management platforms. Thanks to new regulations, the Italian market now has a complete legislative platform with a clear and flexible structure in line with other Western European countries.

Each Italian real estate investment vehicle is analysed in its legal and financial details, providing insight on the management structure, the rights and powers of the investors, the typical investment process and the related costs.

The self-management and external management models, adopted by different investment vehicles, are compared in order to assess their advantages and issues, especially for institutional investors.

The performance measurement of Italian closed-end undertakings in collective investment and the phenomenon of discount to net asset value (NAV) for listed real estate alternative investment funds (AIFs) are also given in-depth examination.

This book provides a guide to selecting the more efficient vehicle for a real estate investment in Italy, allowing readers to understand the upside potential of each instrument in order to achieve the most suitable vehicle matching investment criteria. We believe that the Italian real estate market has significant potential, which institutional investors and asset managers will be able to exploit.

A special thanks goes to Gianni Origoni Grippo Cappelli & Partners (particularly Davide Braghini) and Maisto e Associati (particularly Marco Valdonio and Biagio Izzo) for their legal and tax advice. To conclude, I would like to thank the authors, a University researcher and an expert in the field, who unified a business-like point of view and an academic rigorous approach in order to achieve a comprehensive study of the Italian financial real estate market.

Manfredi Catella
CEO, COIMA RES S.p.A. SIIQ
Milan

1   Real estate market in Italy

The role of the Italian real estate market

The real estate market has always played a key role in capital allocation. Italy is no exception to this rule: about 40.62% of the total wealth of Italian resident investors is allocated to real estate, despite significant differences among the institutional sectors (Table 1.1).

Households and non-profit institutions invest most of their assets in real estate (62.24%), with a prevalence of residential buildings (52.87%). Conversely, non-financial companies allocate 34.03% of their assets (i.e. 55.49% of their non-financial assets) to non-residential buildings, in coherence with their economic model.

The share of financial companies in the real estate market is negligible, a mere 1.15% of the total of this asset class; moreover, buildings represent a tiny fraction of the wealth held by this institutional sector, only 1.63%. On the other hand, these data must not be misinterpreted as a lack of interest from financial companies towards real estate: on the contrary, it is a sign of the relative novelty of financial investment in real estate in Italy.[1]

Government, an institutional sector which includes not only central and local government but also national social security funds, has allocated 38.16% of its assets to real estate, but its share of the total is minimal (4.24%), as a consequence of the process of privatisation of public properties that began in the nineties.

If we move the focus onto the evolution of the roles of the different institutional sectors in the classes of residential and non-residential properties in Italy, we may notice the slow but steady decrease of the share held by government and the corresponding increment in the weight of financial companies, especially in the non-residential class (Tables 1.2 and 1.3).

The evolution of the Italian real estate market can be analysed in depth only if it is disaggregated into its two main sub-markets: property and financial real estate.

Table 1.1 Italian resident institutional sectors: asset allocation at the end of 2013.

Assets Values in EUR million	Total	Non-financial companies	Financial companies	General government	Households and non-profit institutions
Real estate	8,757,402	1,799,055	100,316	371,588	6,486,443
Residential	*6,028,545*	*414,213*	*9,382*	*95,037*	*5,509,913*
Non-residential	*2,472,770*	*1,365,159*	*90,882*	*266,735*	*749,994*
Agricultural land	*256,087*	*19,683*	*52*	*9,816*	*226,536*
Fixed assets other than real estate	886,791	661,257	8,830	119,889	96,815
Financial assets	11,916,591	1,551,632	6,044,512	482,202	3,838,245
Total	*21,560,784*	*4,011,944*	*6,153,658*	*973,679*	*10,421,503*

Assets In % of the Total assets	Total	Non-financial companies	Financial companies	General government	Households and non-profit institutions
Real estate	40.62	44.84	1.63	38.16	62.24
Residential	*27.96*	*10.32*	*0.15*	*9.76*	*52.87*
Non-residential	*11.47*	*34.03*	*1.48*	*27.39*	*7.20*
Agricultural land	*1.19*	*0.49*	*0.00*	*1.01*	*2.17*
Fixed assets other than real estate	4.11	16.48	0.14	12.31	0.93
Financial assets	55.27	38.68	98.23	49.52	36.83
Total	*100.00*	*100.00*	*100.00*	*100.00*	*100.00*

Source: Banca d'Italia (2015b) and ISTAT (2015).

Table 1.2 Italian residential properties and institutional sectors.

Values in EUR million	2005	2006	2007	2008	2009	2010	2011	2012	2013
Non-financial companies	375,473	421,824	458,358	480,212	470,178	461,606	447,515	435,445	414,213
Financial companies	8,033	8,018	7,466	7,650	7,017	7,633	8,956	9,305	9,382
Government	83,522	86,802	89,987	93,655	96,508	99,341	100,335	99,052	95,037
Households and non-profit institutions	4,223,905	4,714,294	5,081,683	5,374,851	5,455,238	5,569,731	5,687,987	5,627,072	5,509,913
In % of the Total	*2005*	*2006*	*2007*	*2008*	*2009*	*2010*	*2011*	*2012*	*2013*
Non-financial companies	8.00	8.06	8.13	8.06	7.80	7.52	7.17	7.06	6.87
Financial companies	0.17	0.15	0.13	0.13	0.12	0.12	0.14	0.15	0.16
Government	1.78	1.66	1.60	1.57	1.60	1.62	1.61	1.61	1.58
Households and non-profit institutions	90.04	90.12	90.14	90.24	90.48	90.74	91.08	91.19	91.40

Source: ISTAT (2015).

Table 1.3 Italian non-residential properties and institutional sectors.

Sectors	2005	2006	2007	2008	2009	2010	2011	2012	2013
Non-financial companies	1,026,246	1,150,049	1,248,846	1,295,504	1,303,380	1,308,338	1,370,412	1,397,684	1,365,159
Financial companies	51,217	55,408	62,969	67,988	74,017	79,836	84,162	87,265	90,882
Government	232,839	243,971	254,849	270,033	279,420	285,223	280,775	273,250	266,735
Households and non-profit institutions	608,072	660,797	708,533	739,260	746,106	755,846	772,397	769,864	749,994
In % of the Total	*2005*	*2006*	*2007*	*2008*	*2009*	*2010*	*2011*	*2012*	*2013*
Non-financial companies	53.50	54.50	54.89	54.60	54.24	53.86	54.65	55.29	55.21
Financial companies	2.67	2.63	2.77	2.87	3.08	3.29	3.36	3.45	3.68
Government	12.14	11.56	11.20	11.38	11.63	11.74	11.20	10.81	10.79
Households and non-profit institutions	31.70	31.31	31.14	31.16	31.05	31.11	30.80	30.45	30.33

Source: ISTAT (2015).

Property real estate

The Italian property market, i.e. the market of direct investment in real estate, has been subject to a moderate increase of current prices since the end of the nineties until 2007–2008. This phenomenon in Italy has not caused a real estate bubble of the same proportions experienced by other EU countries, such as Spain or Ireland, keeping the trend of Italian prices close to the weighted average of the Euro Area (Figure 1.1).

The first signs of crisis in the Italian real estate sector can be traced to the decreasing value added and investments of the economic sector "construction" that took place in 2006.[2] This contraction of the economic environment involved the non-residential buildings (especially infra-structures) at first, and was followed closely by the residential sub-sector. The fragility of the economic and financial structure of Italian construc-tion companies, if compared to their European peers,[3] has caused a surge in defaults. This, in conjunction with the serious funding gap experienced by the Italian banking industry, has forced the banks to apply a credit crunch to the sector. As a consequence, investment in new buildings reached its peak in 2007 and then suffered a constant decline, without any sign of reversal (Figure 1.2). Despite this unprecedented phenomenon, the

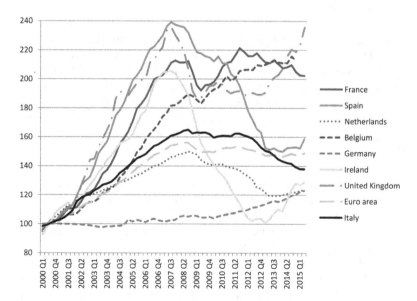

Figure 1.1 House prices in Europe (quarterly data at current values; indices: 2000 = 100).

Source: Banca d'Italia (2015a).

Figure 1.2 Investments in new buildings (millions of euro).

Source: ANCE (2015).

contextual and more than proportional decrease in the number of sales has caused the accumulation of a stock of about half a million unsold houses.[4]

The moderate trend recorded by prices, on the other hand, is not significant if it is not compared to the number of transactions. The volume of real estate sales, in fact, has shrunk during the last decade, partially limiting the significance of the prices, because in a vendor-driven market like the Italian one, properties are exchanged mostly when their price is relatively close to the one asked by the seller.[5]

The index numbers for the prices and amount of sales, disaggregated for property sector, are shown in Figure 1.3. The "double dip" nature of the Italian crisis is clear: after an initial collapse of the volumes in 2008, the market appeared to stabilise in 2009–2011; however, the increasing credit crunch, this time on the buyer side, and the need for Italian banks to close the funding gap caused a new recession in 2012.

The data from recent years, on the other hand, seem to show the beginnings of recovery, probably caused by prices closer to the fundamentals and the affordability of real estate, unprecedented in recent Italian history. This latter aspect is the result of the growth in disposable income, for residential properties, and the improvement in credit conditions. In the second half of 2014 the price-to-rent ratio and has reached a level below its mid- to long-term

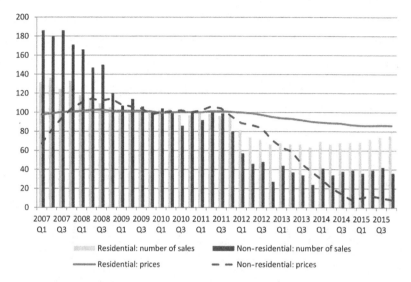

Figure 1.3 Prices and number of sales in the property market.

Source: Banca d'Italia (2016).

average. The affordability indicator, calculated by the Bank of Italy as the ratio of debt service (product of average house prices and interest rates on new mortgages) and households' disposable income, which measures households' access to the property market, has reached its lowest level (i.e. the highest affordability) since 2000 (Figure 1.4).

On a prospective point of view, the intent of Italian families to buy a residential property has been showing a positive trend in 2014–2015, hopefully indicating a reversal of the market, as shown by the "smile" of the interpolating curve of Figure 1.5.

Financial real estate

As will be explained in detail in the following chapters, the three investment vehicles in Italian financial real estate are:

- fondi chiusi immobiliari, i.e. real estate closed-end investment funds;
- SICAF immobiliari, i.e. società di investimento a capitale fisso immobiliari or real estate fixed capital investment companies;
- SIIQ, i.e. società di investimento immobiliare quotate or listed real estate investment companies.

Figure 1.4 Sustainability indicators for the real estate market in Italy.

Source: Banca d'Italia (2016).

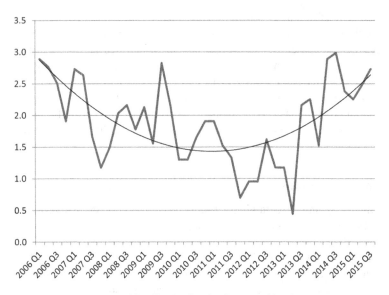

Figure 1.5 Percentage of families inclined to buy a residential property.

Source: ANCE (2015).

Funds and SICAFs are undertakings for collective investment (UCIs), more precisely are alternative investment funds (AIFs), and SIIQs are companies listed on a regulated market.

Although real estate SICAFs were only introduced in 2014, the market of real estate investment funds has already reached its maturity. The process of development of real estate funds has been characterised by a steady and relevant shift from retail to professional investors. While real estate investment funds were created with the aim of favouring the privatisation of government properties, contributed into real estate investment funds, by the placement of funds units to the retail market, today investment funds reserved for professional investors are the most relevant component of this sector, both as number of funds and as aggregate gross asset values (GAVs) and net asset values (NAVs) (Table 1.4). For example, the aggregate NAV of reserved real estate investment funds accounted for 90.5% of the total at the end of 2015 (Figure 1.6).

A comparison of the amount of properties held by funds (Table 1.4) with the total value of real estate in Italy (Table 1.1) reveals the limited role played by financial real estate (a mere 0.55%), despite its substantial growth since 2003 (compound annual growth rate 24.2%). A growth that has been halted by the second stage of the Italian double dip crisis (2011–2012), but this temporary stalemate showed signs of positive reversal in 2014.

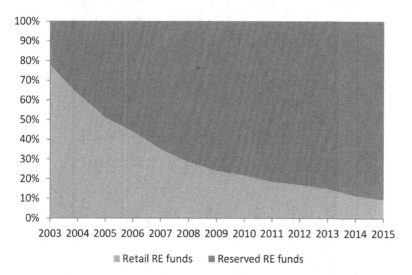

Figure 1.6 Market share of retail and reserved real estate funds, measured by their NAV.

Source: data from Bank of Italy.

Table 1.4 Real estate investment funds.

RE investment funds	2003	2004	2005	2006	2007	2008	2009	2010	2011	2012	2013	2014	2015
Non-reserved													
Number of funds	14	19	23	29	30	29	27	27	28	27	26	27	26
GAV	3,836	6,531	8,057	10,168	10,731	10,185	9,461	9,174	8,523	7,807	7,062	5,776	5,038
of which: properties	*2,847*	*5,105*	*6,407*	*7,935*	*8,900*	*8,577*	*7,971*	*7,566*	*7,198*	*6,660*	*5,986*	*4,658*	*4,109*
Debt	312	1,301	1,797	2,687	2,960	2,983	2,978	2,787	2,501	2,275	1,983	1,286	1,070
NAV	3,425	5,102	6,058	7,211	7,557	6,976	6,307	6,199	5,798	5,347	4,938	4,343	3,846
Leverage (GAV/NAV)	1.12	1.28	1.33	1.41	1.42	1.46	1.50	1.48	1.47	1.46	1.43	1.33	1.31
Reserved													
Number of funds	5	12	38	90	144	200	240	269	301	324	335	368	391
GAV	1,304	5,778	10,269	17,080	25,326	32,204	38,055	41,424	45,089	45,645	48,150	52,591	55,299
of which: properties	*872*	*5,415*	*8,804*	*14,120*	*21,481*	*28,112*	*32,839*	*36,278*	*39,682*	*40,170*	*41,977*	*45,581*	*47,393*
Debt	261	2,678	4,222	7,203	10,494	13,647	16,538	17,373	17,515	17,367	17,837	17,225	16,272
NAV	980	2,978	5,805	9,167	13,966	17,477	19,985	22,435	25,516	26,177	28,099	33,320	36,631
Leverage (GAV/NAV)	1.33	1.94	1.77	1.86	1.81	1.84	1.90	1.85	1.77	1.74	1.71	1.58	1.51
Total													
Number of funds	19	31	61	119	174	229	267	296	329	351	361	395	417
GAV	5,140	12,309	18,326	27,248	36,057	42,389	47,516	50,598	53,612	53,452	55,212	58,367	60,337
of which: properties	*3,719*	*10,520*	*15,211*	*22,055*	*30,381*	*36,689*	*40,810*	*43,844*	*46,880*	*46,830*	*47,963*	*50,239*	*51,502*
Debt	573	3,979	6,019	9,890	13,454	16,630	19,516	20,160	20,016	19,642	19,820	18,511	17,342
NAV	4,405	8,081	11,863	16,378	21,523	24,453	26,292	28,634	31,313	31,524	33,038	37,663	40,477
Leverage (GAV/NAV)	1.17	1.52	1.54	1.66	1.68	1.73	1.81	1.77	1.71	1.70	1.67	1.55	1.49

Balance sheet items in EUR million

Source: data from Bank of Italy.

Due to the recent credit crunch, which has affected real estate more than any other economic sector, leverage has returned to safer levels and now the financial structures of retail and reserved funds are quite close, with leverages (defined here as GAV/NAV) of 1.33 and 1.58 respectively.

Listed real estate companies (SIIQs) are a relative novelty for Italian investors and, as a consequence, their role in this asset class is still limited today, but the initial public offering of COIMA Res SIIQ in May 2016 has renewed the interest of the market in this investment vehicle.

In July 2016 four companies listed on the markets operated by Borsa Italiana SpA had the status of SIIQ and their aggregate capitalisation was equal to about 2.3 billion euro. Their free-float, on the other hand, was far from the minimum required by Italian law for SIIQ status (25%) and equal to about 45%, showing a positive interest of the retail market towards these companies. Among the relevant participants, foreign companies and funds play a key role, with the control of about 47% of the aggregate capital of Italian SIIQs.

Notes

1 The assets of real estate funds are included in the financial companies sector.
2 Gobbi and Zollino (2013).
3 De Socio (2010).
4 No data are available for non-residential buildings, and even for the residential sector estimates vary significantly from a minimum of 400,000 to a maximum of 700,000 houses (Fabrizi et al., 2015).
5 In Italy, unsold buildings owned by companies active in the real estate industry are regarded as inventories and, therefore, are not subject to property taxes.

2   Italian financial real estate from a European perspective

European real estate AIFs

The Alternative Investment Fund Managers Directive (AIFMD) of the European Council and Parliament classifies UCIs in real estate, e.g. real estate (or property) funds, in the category of the AIFs.[1] This legal definition is the reason for the variety in the characteristics of these investment vehicles in different countries, as national regulations are set independently by the respective supervisory authorities.

EU real estate AIFs can be classified into three basic legal structures: the contractual form; the trust form; and the corporate form. National regulations do not always comprise all of them.[2]

In the contractual form, the fund is not a legal entity and, therefore, it must be managed by an Alternative Investment Fund Manager (AIFM), responsible for the administration of the assets and in whose name the AIF's real estate is held, albeit in the form of a separate fund. This is the classical form for common funds in many European countries (Germany, Italy, France, etc.), but it is not entirely suitable for real estate funds, because their assets are non-fungible goods and sometimes they have been contributed by participants who wish to retain a certain level of discretion in their management.

In the trust form, a portfolio of assets is constituted and managed by the trustee (always an AIFM, in the EU) on behalf of the beneficiaries, i.e. the investors in the fund. The trust form is typical of countries of Anglo-Saxon law and, as for the contractual form, the separation between investors and management may not always be the best solution for real estate funds.

The AIF established in corporate form, instead, is a legal entity and the investors are its shareholders. The governance model adopted by this form is similar to that of a joint-stock company, and the ordinary shareholders have full rights in the definition of the investment policies applied by the administrative body, which can be either internal or externalised to an AIFM. Different types of shares, with limited administrative rights, may also be issued, which would differentiate shareholders according to their objectives:

either control of a property, favouring the possibility to hold voting rights, or mere financial investment, without interferences in management policy. Moreover, the assets of a fund set as a legal entity can be assigned directly to the fund itself, providing a higher level of transparency both for shareholders and other stakeholders. The latter can include the credit sector, which can easily assess the real estate portfolio of an individual AIF separately from that of other ones promoted by the same AIFM.

Different institutional models can be classified also according to their specific economic features. A first distinction regards the timing of investors' right to subscribe and redeem units or shares. Notwithstanding the fact that real estate assets are inherently illiquid, open-end real estate funds are allowed by the legislation of some of the main European countries (e.g., Germany). Due to the illiquidity of real assets, open-end real estate funds must always keep a liquidity cushion, and national legislation may prevent reimbursement if requests are such as to undermine the solvency of the fund.[3] In order to mitigate further the liquidity risk, the funds may also be semi-open-end, in which case reimbursements are possible only in given time periods.

With more coherence to the illiquidity of their assets, real estate funds can be closed-end. Like in all closed-end funds, where units cannot be issued or reimbursed after the establishment of the fund, real estate funds must also be liquidated by a date specified in the regulations and coherently with the stated investment policies. Due to the complexity of the liquidation of relevant properties, especially if the sector is suffering a crisis, their maturity (usually less than 50 years) can be extended for a period of some years, known as the grace period. In order to allow unitholders to sell their investment, closed-end funds may be listed on a regulated market (listed funds). Funds can also be established in the hybrid semi-closed-end form. These funds can accept new subscriptions on certain pre-set dates and, at the same time, they offer the opportunity for early redemption of, at most, a comparable sum.

Real estate funds can be retail, if targeted indistinctively at investors, or reserved, if intended for qualifying investors only. The most relevant difference between the two categories involves the constraints that may be placed on the asset allocation, which usually serve three purposes. The first is to guarantee a coherent asset allocation policy, by requiring that the majority of assets be in the form of real estate, with the remaining part linked to the real estate market, like shareholdings in real estate companies or securities backed by leased properties or by mortgages. A further constraint requires a minimum level of investment diversification, in order to reduce the exposure to idiosyncratic risk. The third constraint is applied on leverage, aimed at avoiding excessive debt.

The last two rules apply only in part, if at all, to qualifying investor funds, for which lawmakers have assumed that protection can be less stringent. In particular, the requirement for a minimum diversification is always loosened or even absent, because qualifying investors frequently use real estate funds to manage a limited number of major operations, in which the value added is sought precisely in the manager's specialisation in a specific real estate sector.

Table 2.1 summarises the characteristics of funds focused on direct investment in real estate in the main markets of the European Union.

European REITs

The US Real estate investment trust (REIT) has been the paradigm for EU national regulations for the definition of the characteristics of companies dedicated exclusively to the investment in real estate through the collection of savings from the public.[4] Despite the name, a US-REIT is not always set up as a trust, but can also be a company or an association with at least 100 shareholders (or beneficiaries in the case of a trust) and is not closely held, i.e. no more than 50% of its outstanding stock is owned, directly or indirectly, by or for not more than five individuals.[5] US-REITs benefit from special tax regulations, thanks to their status of pass-through entities, and are not liable to tax on the profits distributed to shareholders, which must be at least 90% of the taxable income.

Based on the US experience, several EU countries have introduced fiscal regimes comparable to the US-REITs. In 1969, for the first time in Europe, the Netherlands instituted tax exempt companies known as "Fiscale beleggingsinstelling" (FBI), while Belgium introduced the "Sociétés d'investissement à capital fixe immobilière" in 1995, which was then replaced by the "Sociétés immobilières réglementées" (SIR) in 2014. In 2003, the "Sociétés d'investissement immobilier cotées" (SIIC) were defined by the French law, while in 2007 the regulations on the "Società di investimento immobiliare quotate" (SIIQ) in Italy and the "Real estate investment trusts" in the United Kingdom and Germany were approved. In order to distinguish the British and German vehicles from the US model, the acronyms UK-REIT and G-REIT are of widespread use.

National regulations in the EU exempt REITs from income tax, making them pass-through entities but, in order to avoid an indefinite deferral of income tax, European REITs are required to distribute a significant portion of their net profits, which are then taxed on the REIT shareholders.

As in the USA, national regulations in the EU require that companies satisfy certain requirements in order to benefit from the REIT tax regime (Table 2.2). With the only exception of the FBIs in the Netherlands,

Table 2.1 Real estate AIFs in the main European markets.

Country	Real estate fund	Closed-end/ Open-end	Legal entity	Investors	Main investment constraints
France	Organisme de Placement Collectif en Immobilier (OPCI)	Open-end	No	Retail	≥ 60% in real estate, ≥ 5% in liquid assets, diversification
	Fonds de placement immobilier (FPI)				
	Société de placement à prépondérance immobilière à capital variable (SPPICAV)	Open-end	Yes	Retail	≥ 60% in real estate, ≥ 5% in liquid assets, diversification
	Organisme professionnel de placement collectif en immobilier (OPPCI)	Open-end	No	Qualified	≥ 60% in real estate, ≥ 5% in liquid assets
	Fonds professionnel de placement immobilier (FPPI)				
	Société professionnel de placement à prépondérance immobilière à capital variable (SPPPICAV)	Open-end	Yes	Qualified	≥ 60% in real estate, ≥ 5% in liquid assets
Germany	"Offen Immobilienfonds"	Open-end	No	Retail	≥ 51% in real estate, ≥ 5% in liquid assets, diversification
	Immobilien-Sondervermögen				
	Immobilien-Spezial-Sondervermögen	Open-end	No	Qualified	≥ 51% in real estate, ≥ 5% in liquid assets, diversification
	"Geschlossen Immobilienfonds"	Closed-end	Yes	Retail	Diversification
	Immobilien Investment-KG				
	Immobilien Spezial-Investment-KG	Closed-end	Yes	Qualified	
Italy	Fondo chiuso immobiliare	Closed-end or semi-closed-end	No	Retail	≥ 66,67% in real estate, diversification
	Fondo d'investimento alternativo immobiliare				
	Società di investimento a capitale fisso immobiliare (SICAF immobiliare)	Closed-end or semi-closed-end	Yes	Retail	≥ 66,67% in real estate, diversification

(continued)

Table 2.1 (continued)

Country	Real estate fund		Closed-end/ Open-end	Legal entity	Investors	Main investment constraints
	Fondo d'investimento alternativo immobiliare riservato	Fondo chiuso immobiliare riservato	Closed-end or semi-closed-end	No	Qualified	≥ 66,67% in real estate
		Società di investimento a capitale fisso immobiliare riservata (SICAF immobiliare riservata)	Closed-end or semi-closed-end	Yes	Qualified	≥ 66,67% in real estate
	Organisme de placement collectif (2010 Partie II)	Fonds commun de placement (FCP)	Closed-, semi-open- or open-end	No	Retail	Diversification
		Société d'investissement à capital variable (SICAV)	Closed-, semi-open- or open-end	Yes	Retail	Diversification
		Société d'investissement à capital fixe (SICAF)	Closed-, semi-open- or open-end	Yes	Retail	Diversification
Luxembourg	Fonds d'investissement spécialisé	Fonds commun de placement (FCP)	Closed-, semi-open- or open-end	No	Qualified	Diversification (with exceptions subject to authorisation)
		Société d'investissement à capital variable (SICAV)	Closed-, semi-open- or open-end	Yes	Qualified	Diversification (with exceptions subject to authorisation)
		Société d'investissement à capital fixe (SICAF)	Closed-, semi-open- or open-end	Yes	Qualified	Diversification (with exceptions subject to authorisation)
	Société d'investissement en capital à risque (SICAR)		Closed-, semi-open- or open-end	Yes	Qualified	Investment only in property companies
	Non-UCITS retail scheme (NURS)	Authorised property unit trust (APUT)	Open-end	No	Retail	Diversification
		Property authorised investment trust (PAIF) – NURS	Open-end	Yes	Retail	≥ 60% in real estate or listed REIT shares, diversification
United Kingdom	Qualified investor scheme (QIS)	Unauthorised property unit trust (UPUT)	Open-end	No	Qualified	
		Property authorised investment trust (PAIF) – QIS	Open-end	Yes	Qualified	≥ 60% in real estate or listed REIT shares

Source: Adapted from Basile and Ferrari (2016).

Table 2.2 REITs in the main European markets.

Country	National "REIT"	Main requirements						
		Listing mandatory	Shareholders	Asset allocation	Activity	Debt	Income distribution
Belgium	Société immobilière réglementée (SIR)	Yes	None	≤ 20% in a single asset	Development and property management (no delegations allowed)	≤ 65% of total assets	≥ 80% of net income
France	Société d'investissement immobilier cotée (SIIC)	Yes	Free float ≥ 15%. Single shareholder ≤ 60%	Principally leased real estate	Leasing must be the principal activity	No limits	≥ 95% of net income from leasing activity; ≥ 60% of capital gains; 100% of dividends
Germany	Real-Estate-Investment-Trust (G-REIT)	Yes	Free float ≥ 15%. Single shareholder ≤ 10%	Real estate ≥ 75%	Revenues from lease activity ≥ 75%	Equity ≥ 45% of real estate assets	≥ 90% of net income; 50% of capital gains can be transferred to reserve
Italy	Società d'investimento immobiliare quotata (SIIQ)	Yes	Free float ≥ 25%. Single shareholder ≤ 60%	Leased real estate ≥ 80%	Revenues from lease activity ≥ 80%	Limited by company bylaws	≥ 70% of the lower between net income from leasing activity and total net income; 50% of capital gains (during the following 2 years)

(continued)

Table 2.2 (continued)

Country	National "REIT"	Main requirements					
		Listing mandatory	Shareholders	Asset allocation	Activity	Debt	Income distribution
Netherlands	Fiscale beleggingsinstelling (FBI)	No	If listed: Single shareholder ≤ 45% (if company) or 25% (if individual) If unlisted: individuals or non-taxable corporations or FBIs ≥ 75%. Single shareholder ≤ 5%	Only passive portfolio investments	Leasing must be the main activity	≤ 60% of tax book value of direct/indirect real estate and ≤ 20% of tax book value of other assets	100% of taxable income; capital gains/losses can be allocated to a tax-free reserve
United Kingdom	Real estate investment trust (UK-REIT)	Yes	Free float ≥ 35%. Single shareholder ≤ 10%	Leased real estate ≥ 75%; ≤ 40% in a single asset	Revenues from lease activity ≥ 75%	Property incomes must be ≥ 1.25 times the property financing costs	≥ 90% of net income from lease activity; 100% of dividends from another REIT

Source: Adapted from Basile and Ferrari (2016).

the listing on a regulated market is a fundamental requirement for European REITs, because they are instruments conceived to facilitate the access of retail investors to the real estate market. In order to ensure a broad-based share ownership, moreover, there may be a required minimum of floating stock, or constraints on the maximum holdings allowed for a limited number of subjects. REITs are also subject to the so-called asset test, i.e. the asset allocation must comply with certain constraints, usually regarding the prevalence of investment in the space market and/or portfolio diversification. In line with the composition of the assets and in order to satisfy the requirement known as income test, income must derive mostly from rents.

The degree of leverage that can be taken by REITs is subject to different regulations in the EU. In some countries, e.g. France and Italy, REITs have free recourse to leverage, as is the case with companies active in different economic sectors.[6] When, instead, the protection of retail investors is regarded as more relevant, the leverage or gearing ratio, usually calculated as a ratio to specific categories of assets, is constrained. The UK-REITs are the only exception to these two models of regulation, because their leverage constraint is proportional to profitability: in order to pass the interest cover test, profits deriving from properties cannot be less than 1.25 times the interest on liabilities contracted for the investment in real assets. This rule, albeit apparently rational from an economic point of view, can be a source of risk for the UK-REITs if variable interest rate debts are contracted at a time of particularly low rates. Should interest rates rise significantly, in fact, the failure to comply with the constraint would cause a strong deleveraging, with a predictable impact on the selling price of the liquidated properties.

Italian real estate management companies and the AIFMD

Prior to the AIFMD,[7] issued in 2011, no common framework for alternative, i.e. non-UCITS, collective investments vehicles existed in the European Union. In order to leave the maximum flexibility to national authorities with regards to the definition of the alternative investment vehicles, the AIFMD focuses solely on AIFMs.

In Italy, real estate AIFs are established and managed by firms providing investment services named Società di gestione del risparmio (SGR), i.e. asset management companies (AMC),[8] which, under the scope of AIFMD, must comply with the requirements imposed to AIFMs, i.e. gestori di fondi di investimento alternativi (GEFIA).

The asset management company, in compliance with Council Directive 93/22/EEC of 10 May 1993 and with Italian Legislative Decree no. 58 of 24 February 1998 named Testo Unico della Finanza (TUF),[9] has to be authorised by the Bank of Italy and to obtain such authorisation it must comply with the following requirements:

- legal form as a società per azioni, i.e. an Italian joint-stock company;
- registered office and head office located in Italy;
- minimum paid-up capital according to the rules established by the Bank of Italy;
- special requirements of professionalism, integrity, independence, competence and fairness for the persons performing administrative, management and control functions;
- requirements of integrity and the ability to meet criteria of competence and fairness so as to ensure the sound and prudent management of the investee company for shareholders;
- structure of the group, of which the company is part, that is not prejudicial to the controls by the competent authorities and to the effective supervision of the company;
- audited financial statements;
- submission to the Bank of Italy and to Consob of the following documents: a programme of initial operations, a description of the organisational structure, the articles of association and the bylaws of the company;
- company name containing the words SGR.

When the above-mentioned requirements are fulfilled, the Bank of Italy, after consulting Consob, authorises the asset management company to provide the collective asset management services. Upon the authorisation, the Bank of Italy enters the asset management company in a public register, according to art. 35, paragraph 1 of the TUF.

Most of the Italian AMCs specialising in real estate funds have their origin in a real estate company, while only about one quarter have a banking or financial background. Usually the Italian management companies with the most "technical" background have a wide knowledge of the management of real estate properties, focusing on development and refurbishment/optimisation of buildings, while management companies with a "financial" background focus on funds invested in assets with ongoing cash flows.

According to art. 41 of TUF, an Italian authorised management company can operate in another EU member state either with or without the establishment of a branch, under the principle of freedom to provide services. Similarly, according to art. 41-ter of TUF, foreign AMCs authorised in their EU home country as AIFMs may provide the same asset management services in Italy on a cross-border basis. Only a prior notification to the Bank of Italy is required in order to carry out asset management services in Italy.

Above all, the competent authority of the EU home country must inform the Bank of Italy, which will promptly forward such communication to the Consob. Further specific requirements apply for EU managers wanting to manage an Italian AIF, i.e. the EU managers must be authorised to manage AIFs of a similar nature in their home country.

On the other hand, non-EU AIFMs interested in managing or marketing Italian or other EU AIFs in EU countries have to be authorised by the Bank of Italy, after consultation with Consob. This is similar to the Italian SGR authorisation process. However, if non-EU AIFMs have already been authorised in another EU country, they can follow the above-mentioned notification process under art. 41-ter of the TUF related to EU AIFMs.

EU and non-EU AIFMs operating in Italy through a branch must comply with all Italian laws and regulations, including conduct rules, conflict of interest provisions and the disclosure requirements prescribed to Italian managers. Capital requirements and supervision for the AIFMs are regulated by the home country legislation.

The marketing in Italy of fund units/shares of a EU real estate AIF managed by an EU asset management company requires a prior notification to the Consob of all the details about the AIF to be marketed.

Notes

1 Directive 2011/61/EU of the European Parliament and of the Council of 8 June 2011 on AIFMs. According to Article 4(1)(a): "AIFs means collective investment undertakings, including investment compartments thereof, which: (i) raise capital from a number of investors, with a view to investing it in accordance with a defined investment policy for the benefit of those investors; and (ii) do not require authorisation pursuant to Article 5 of Directive 2009/65/EC."
2 Basile and Ferrari (2016).
3 For example, the German Immobilien-Sondervermögen (commonly known as Offene Immobilienfonds) must hold liquid assets equal to at least 5% of their GAV, moreover, the fund can suspend redemptions in times of crisis. Breuer and Nadler (2012), Just and Maenning (2012).
4 Sotelo and McGreal (2013).
5 United States Code, Title 26, § 856.
6 Morri and Artegiani (2015).
7 Directive 2011/61/EU.
8 For an analysis of Italian AMCs specialised in real estate funds, see Abate (2011).
9 The TUF is the Consolidated Law on Finance that regulates important issues of Italian securities law.

3 Real estate investment funds

Regulatory framework

Real estate investment funds were introduced in Italy by Law no. 86 on 25 January 1994 and, after several amendments, only art. 14-bis of Law 86/1994, related to public contribution funds, is still in force. The main amendments were introduced by Law Decree no. 78 on 31 May 2010, and subsequently converted by Law no. 122 on 13 May 2011, primarily related to the tax regime of funds.

In 2014 and 2015 the Bank of Italy and the Italian Ministry of Economy and Finance (MEF) introduced new rules, transposing the AIFMD into Italian legislation.[1] According to the current regulatory framework, real estate investment funds belong to the category of AIFs and their management must be carried out, in the interest of the investors participating in the fund but independently of them, by an AIFM, i.e. Gestore di fondi di investimento alternativi (GEFIA), an asset management company (AMC), i.e. Società di gestione del risparmio (SGR), that qualifies as an AIFM.

The Italian law "Testo unico della finanza" (TUF),[2] i.e. Consolidated Law on Finance, allows us to define an investment fund as:

- a fund constituted as an autonomous capital, which is not a legal entity;
- subdivided in units/shares with equal value;
- instituted and managed by an asset management company;
- representing a scheme established with the aim of a collective asset management, whose assets are raised from a plurality of investors, by means of issue or offer of units;
- managed on a collective basis in the interests of the investors and autonomously from the same and invested in financial instruments, receivables, interest or transferable or immovable properties, according to a prearranged investment strategy.

These delimitations outline the following main requirements:

- collection of the capital from a plurality of investors;[3]
- existence of an investment strategy defined in advance;
- management that is independent of the participants in the funds;
- separation of fund assets from those of the AMC, of the other funds and of the participants.

More in detail, according to art. 12 of the MEF Decree no. 30 of 5 March 2015, a real estate investment fund:

- is set up only as a closed-end fund with the right of reimbursement for the investors at established times of payment;
- invests at least two-thirds of its GAV in real estate properties, real estate rights and shareholdings in real estate companies. This limit is reduced to 51% when at least 20% of the assets are invested into financial instruments deriving from securitisation of real estate assets, property rights or receivables secured by real estate mortgages.

The AIFM must comply with all the requirements in the start-up phase as well as during the life of the fund. All the rules and specifications are displayed in the fund rules (regolamento del fondo), i.e. the terms and conditions settled by the AIFM in compliance with existing European and Italian legal provisions.

Fund capital is divided into units, each one being of equal value, and the subscription period has to be specified in the fund rules. The maximum subscription period for closed-end funds is 24 months from the positive conclusion of the marketing notification process with Consob[4] or, with reference to listed funds, from the publication of the fund prospectus. Only a postponement of 12 months is allowed. A reopening of subscriptions is possible if allowed by the fund rules.

The fund rules also establish the details and schemes of:

- partial reimbursements (pro quota) in case of divestments;
- anticipated reimbursement (pro quota) in case of divestments or in case of new issues of units;
- subsequent issues of units.

Each real estate fund, due to its closed-end nature, can issue a predetermined number of units defined during the start-up phase in accordance with fund market strategy. Units can have different classes, based on the needs of the specific investors to whom the shares are to be sold. Different unit classes within the same fund are typically created in order to confer different rights to their owners (i.e., Class A units reserved to institutional investors vs. Class B issued to other investors). Further issues of units after the first one are allowed.

The real estate investment fund is not a legal entity under Italian law, instead it is an independent pool of assets managed on a collective basis by an AMC (Figure 3.1). Nevertheless, each pool of assets is legally segregated from other pools of assets managed by the same company. Moreover, fund assets are separated from those of the management company itself, as well as from the assets of the unitholders. The AMC entirely segregates the fund assets from any other assets and establishes a separate local bank account in the name of each fund that is managed by it. The asset management company acts as a self-governing and independent decision maker on behalf of the investors. It is to be noted that the asset management company retains control over the fund as well as the predominance in the definition of the investment strategy.

The unitholders meeting, which is the collective organism representing the interests of participants in a real estate investment fund, has the right to: provide guidelines to the asset management policies, modify the fund rules,

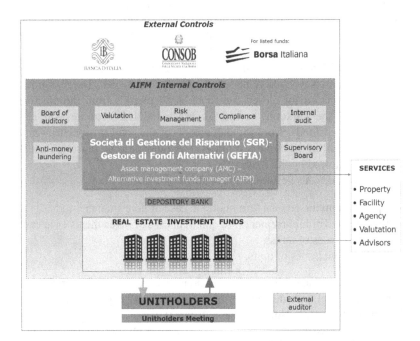

Figure 3.1 Structure of a real estate fund.

deliberate the early liquidation of the fund and, its most relevant power, appoint a new AMC if the current one does not satisfy investors' objectives.

In cases where the assets of the fund do not meet the obligations towards third parties and there is no reasonable prospect that this situation can be overcome, the AMC itself or one or more creditors may request the forced liquidation of the fund at a court of the district where the AMC has its registered office. In cases of fund default or other unfulfilled conditions, the Bank of Italy may require supervision by an external commissioner and declare the forced sale of the fund assets as well as the subsequent liquidation of the fund.

According to art. 6 of the MEF Decree no. 30 of 5 March 2015, the maximum term of a real estate investment fund is 50 years. The fund rules establish the maturity and the right to postpone this term. The fund rules may also provide that the AMC can postpone the term in order to complete the liquidation of the fund's properties. In this case the maximum postponement period allowed is 3 years (the so-called "grace period").

The main documents that the fund must provide to investors are:

- fund rules (regolamento del fondo), defining in detail the fund terms and conditions;
- general journal (libro giornale), a document in which the asset manager records, day by day, all the management activities and the eventual reimbursements of units;
- management report (relazione degli amministratori), containing a description of the main management operations;
- management report of the fund (rendiconto di gestione del fondo), to be produced within 60 days of the end of each financial period or at the time of the distribution of proceeds;
- half-year report (relazione semestrale), including the asset valuation with descriptive notes, to be produced within 30 days from the end of the first half of the year;
- unit value (valore della quota), a prospect analysing the value of each unit, to be produced at the reimbursement of units.

Italian real estate investment funds can be classified according to different criteria (Figure 3.2). With regards to the type of participants, funds can be reserved or non-reserved to qualifying investors. The former ones are exclusively designed for institutional and professional qualified investors with financial experience, while the latter ones are open to every type of investor.

A further taxonomy regards the initial contribution to the fund by investors. Italian real estate funds may be set up by contribution or partial contribution of assets (fondi immobiliari ad apporto) or by capital contribution (fondi immobiliari ordinari).

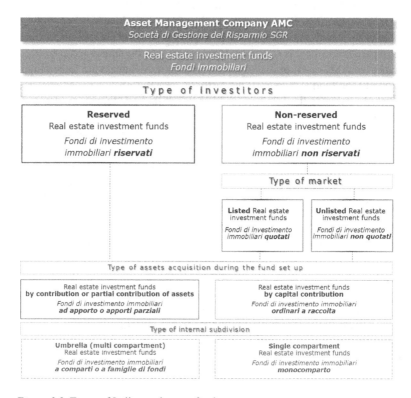

Figure 3.2 Types of Italian real estate funds.

Contribution funds are set up through partial or total contribution of assets, represented by real estate, real property rights or investments in real estate companies, in exchange for units of the fund itself. The operation of assets contribution requires an appraisal (a valuation report) carried out by an external valuer, i.e. an independent expert, in order to ensure a valuation at market prices of the assets transferred to the fund. The valuation report has to be carried out no earlier than 30 days before the contribution of the assets and the total value of units issued after the contribution must not exceed the value of the goods, as certified in the appraisal report.

The fund rules contain the obligation for the contributors of properties to integrate these assets with a capital contribution of at least 5% of the assets value. This liquidity derived from compulsory contributions in cash cannot be used for the acquisition of real estate or real estate rights; an exception is possible only in cases in which purchases of real estate are strictly necessary to pursue the fund strategy, providing that such purchases involve an investment of no more than 30% of the total liquidity contributed.

Contribution funds that have been set up by public entities (fondi immobiliari ad apporto pubblico) are subject to specific rules.[5] Their primary aim is that of privatising the real estate assets contributed to the fund, and therefore the asset management company is required to sell on the market at least 60% of the fund units. If this target is not reached within 18 months, the fund must be liquidated.

Focusing on the structure of the fund, it can be organised as a single fund (monocomparto) or as an umbrella or multi compartment fund (multicomparto), i.e. a fund adopting a multilevel structure including a series of sub-funds. The strategy of this latter type of funds is to establish several investment objectives under the same investment vehicle. Each sub-fund has different investment policies, terms and conditions, providing several allocation choices to investors.

The multi compartment structure gives the possibility to separate investors into specific sub-funds, each one with its own investment properties and related income. For example, an umbrella fund may invest in the same asset class (e.g. retail parks) but within a different Italian region for each sub-fund, offering units of the sub-funds to different investors interested in a particular region, but not in the remaining ones.

Moreover, sub-funds may be set up on different dates and with different maturities. In principle, the switch of units from one-sub fund to another within the same umbrella fund may be carried out easily and at a lower cost. The fund rules are composed of a main general part and a second part describing product characteristics subdivided for each sub-fund. Unitholders' meetings are divided in two meetings: one for the main fund and one for each sub fund.

It is common practice for Italian AIFMs to market real estate fund families of funds (famiglie di fondi) or funds systems (sistemi di fondi). They adopt a structure similar to the above-mentioned umbrella funds, but with unitary rules containing common predictions for a family of different funds, with only some articles devoted to each one of them.

Asset allocation and leverage

As stated above, a real estate fund must invest at least two-thirds of its GAV in real estate properties, real estate rights and shareholdings in real estate companies. The investment limit is reduced to 51% when at least 20% of the assets are invested in financial instruments deriving from securitisation of real estate, property rights or receivables secured by real estate mortgages. These requirements have to be fulfilled within 24 months of the establishment of the fund, while funds investing in residential social housing are allowed to comply with the limits within 48 months.

Table 3.1 Limits imposed to real estate funds.

	Non-reserved real estate funds fondi immobiliari non riservati	*Reserved real estate funds* fondi immobiliari riservati
Asset allocation	Non-reserved real estate funds cannot invest directly, or through subsidiaries, more than 20% in a single building with unitary use, zoning and characteristics that can be considered marketable on a single unit basis. This concentration limit is increased to 33% in case of buildings that have rental purpose and the main tenant (including tenants owned by the main tenant) produces revenues exceeding 20% of the total yearly rents of the same asset. Furthermore, non-reserved real estate funds cannot invest more than 10% of their assets in shares issued by the same construction company.	Reserved real estate funds do not provide for prudential rules if not stated within the fund rules. They have looser restrictions compared to listed funds because it is assumed that their unitholders are experienced investors. For instance, they can allocate more than one third of their assets in just one property and no more than 10% of shares issued by the same construction company. In terms of conflict of interest, there are no limits regarding investment acquisitions by the owners and shareholders of the asset management company or by companies that are part of the holding group owner or partial owner in the asset management company, but a direct or indirect investment in assets owned by a manager, general manager or a board member is not allowed.
Leverage	Non-reserved real estate funds can borrow directly or through subsidiaries if the overall exposure does not exceed a leverage of 2, calculated in compliance with Chapter II, Section 2 of Commission Delegated Regulation (EU) No 231/2013.	According to current Italian rules there is not a specific limit for reserved real estate funds with regard to total exposure. The leverage ratio of each fund has to be disclosed to the Bank of Italy in addition to the relevant information about the fund. The Bank of Italy can impose limits if leverage is deemed unsustainable.

With reference to concentration risk (Table 3.1), non-reserved real estate funds cannot invest directly or through subsidiaries more than 20% of their assets in a single property with unitary use, zoning and characteristics that can be considered marketable on a single unit basis. This concentration limit is increased to 33% in the case of buildings that have a rental purpose and the main tenant (including further tenants owned by the main tenant) produces rents/revenues exceeding 20% of the total yearly rents of the same asset.

A periodical review of the above-mentioned concentration limits must take into account the initial subscriptions and the partial repayments made by the fund in favour of all the participants in proportion to the value of the units held by them.

Investment in construction companies, whether direct or through subsidiaries, is limited to 10% of the total assets of the real estate fund.

Concerning real estate funds reserved to qualifying investors, no limitation is required by existing laws (Table 3.1); however, portfolio diversification has to be taken into account in order to decrease concentration risk and investment limits have to be specified in the fund rules. With regards to the regulation of conflicts of interests in reserved funds, there are no limits regarding investment acquisitions by the owners and shareholders of the asset management company or by companies that are part of the holding group owner or partial owner of the asset management company, even though a direct or indirect investment, by the fund, of assets owned by a manager, general manager or a board member is not allowed.

The fund can borrow according to a specified leverage ratio, suitable for the fund's purposes. According to current Italian rules there is not a specific limit for real estate funds, excluding non-reserved real estate funds. The leverage ratio of each fund must be specified in the fund rules and has to be disclosed to the Bank of Italy in addition to any other relevant information; the Bank of Italy has the power to request the introduction of limits if leverage is considered not sustainable.

Non-reserved real estate funds, instead, cannot borrow, or have at any given time borrowings, directly or through subsidiaries, to the extent that the overall exposure of the fund (including derivatives) exceeds two times the NAV. In other words, the overall leverage of a non-reserved real estate fund must be calculated as a ratio between the exposure of the fund and its NAV and must be lower than two. In addition to this limit, real estate funds are allowed to borrow temporarily within a limit of 10% of the NAV only in case of anticipated reimbursements.

The EU Commission Delegated Regulation no. 231/2013 has set out two methods to calculate the fund's exposure: the gross method and the commitment method. The gross method calculates the overall exposure of the fund whereas the commitment method gives insight in the hedging and netting techniques employed by the manager. As a consequence, both methods must be used jointly by the asset management company and neither of the two leverage ratios can be above the limit.

The maximum leverage has to be set by the management company and disclosed within the fund rules as well as the extent of the right to reuse collateral or guarantees that shall be granted under the leveraging arrangement. The real estate investment fund must comply with the leverage limits at all times.

The asset management company distributes the fund's profits to the unitholders according to the fund rules; in other words, profits may be periodically distributed or accumulated and distributed only at fund liquidation. There is no legal obligation to provide yearly profit distribution.

Main revenues, costs and fees

Revenues and costs

With reference to real estate funds investing in core and core plus assets, acquired for the cash flows deriving from the rented properties, Table 3.2 provides a summary of the general terms of the main Italian lease agreements concerning commercial properties.

It should be noted that the Law Decree no. 133 of 12 September 2014 has liberalised non-residential property lease agreements with a yearly rent higher than 250,000 euro. This new free form of contract requires an agreement upon:

- the term of the contract, that can be shorter than the minimum term provided by the pre-existing law;
- an increase of the rent, which is not connected only to indexation;
- clauses on the right of withdrawal, indemnity for loss of goodwill, sublease and assignment of the lease agreement, pre-emption right, release, etc.

The above-mentioned free form of lease agreement is applicable only for lease contracts in a written form and for buildings that do not qualify as "historical buildings."

In addition, retail units and other commercial buildings can be subject to a business lease (affitto d'azienda), i.e. a lease of a going concern, business or branch that gives to a party the right to operate it for a certain period. The going concern, business or branch may include, among other assets (i.e. furniture or plants), the right to use and occupy a property to be used primarily for business (i.e. shops or restaurants). An agreement for the lease of a business is more flexible than a property lease. Even though it is governed by a well-defined set of mandatory provisions stated by the Italian Civil Code, the parties have greater autonomy and more freedom to negotiate and to choose the terms of their contract, including how to calculate the rent and its adjustment throughout the term of the lease.

In addition to the revenues deriving from renting, the economic profile of real estate funds is subject to several different sources of revenues and costs, as shown in detail by Table 3.3.

The role played by each item in Table 3.3 changes according to the stage of the fund, given the pre-defined life-span of real estate funds. Table 3.4 provides an overview of the main sources of revenues and costs in each of the main stages of business of real estate funds.

Table 3.2 Main terms of lease agreements of commercial properties.

Use	Typical lease length	Security of occupation after 1st lease expiry	Rent indexation	Maintenance costs
Retail, Office, Storage	6 years	Extension for a further 6 years by automatic renewal, unless a written prior notice is provided by the tenant or (on very limited grounds) the landlord.	Indexed annually to 75% or 100% of consumer index named FOI (famiglie degli operai e impiegati – families of workers and clerks), recorded by ISTAT. Parties may agree on turnover rents (usually in retail units).	Tenant bears minor maintenance costs (ordinary maintenance, i.e., elevator maintenance, etc.). Landlord has duty to make all repairs necessary to maintain the property in good condition (extraordinary maintenance, i.e., roof, external walls, etc.).
Hotel, Theatre, Multiplex	9 years	Extension for a further 9 years by automatic renewals unless a written prior notice given by tenant or landlord (on very limited grounds).	Indexed annually to 75% or 100% of consumer index named FOI. Parties may agree on turnover rents.	See above.

Fees

AMCs charge to the fund the fees related to their management activity performed on behalf of the fund itself. These fees are described in detail within the fund rules and are not subject to value added tax (VAT). The methods of calculation of the fees have to be stated clearly within the fund rules.

In Italy, fees for administration, compliance, distribution, marketing, services to unitholders, record-keeping and other costs for the management of real estate funds vary significantly. There are different approaches to

Table 3.3 Main revenues and costs of rented properties for real estate funds.

Income	
Gross rental income	See Table 3.1.
Gain/(loss) on sales	Gain/loss on sales of properties.

Asset related operating expenses	
Registration tax	Between 0.5% and 2% of the total amount of the rents, referred to the whole lease period. Fixed amount of EUR 200 in the case of financial lease of buildings.
Stamp duty	Not significant. EUR 16 for every four written pages of the contract.
VAT on rents	Lease contracts are signed by the AMC on behalf of each fund, therefore they fall within the scope of VAT but the taxable company subject to VAT is the AMC itself.

Other expenses	
Brokerage fees on new rent contracts	Approximately 10% of first annual rent.
Insurance	Insurance premiums depending on the building replacement costs and on the yearly amount of potential rent loss.
Property taxes	The main municipal taxes related to properties have been encased under the single definition of Imposta Unica Comunale (IUC), a municipal tax. This tax is composed of the three rates: IMU, TASI, TARI. Different types of property are subject to distinct tax rates.
Property management fees	Between 0.80% and 2.5% of annual rents for tenants management plus a mark up on maintenance costs for the facility management services.
Non-recoverable service charges + contingency	i.e. costs for vacant units, legal fees, etc. May include all the costs normally charged on the tenants i.e. fixed and common expenses for the properties located within condominiums.
Capex or maintenance	Depending on age and state of repair of the buildings.
VAT on expenses	The taxable entity subject to VAT is the AMC itself on behalf of the fund. In certain cases VAT may be non-deductible.

TOTAL Asset related operating expenses	
Net rental income	Gross rental income less total asset related operating expenses.
Net financial income	Bank interest and fees.

Net income before taxation

Fund expenses	
Fixed management fee	See Table 3.5.
External valuers for appraisals	Fees are generally calculated on size and use of the buildings. They are usually between 0.005% and 0.040% of GAV.
Depositary bank fee	Fees can vary within a range of 0.020% to 0.080% of GAV.
Other fees (auditors, valuers, etc.)	Variable fees can range from 0.010% to 0.070% of GAV.
VAT on fees	The taxable entity subject to VAT is the AMC itself on behalf of the fund.
Financing costs	Cost of debt depends on the effective rate that the fund pays on debts and on their amount. These costs can be affected by the asset class used as collateral (riskier or speculative) credit ratings of the AMC, size, duration, etc. Other costs related to fund raising, bank relationships and other administrative costs concern the AMC.
VAT credit	The taxable entity subject to VAT is the SGR itself on behalf of the fund.
VAT compensation	*The taxable entity subject to VAT is the AMC itself on behalf of the fund.*
Performance fee (AMC)	*See Table 3.5.*

the computation of annual asset/portfolio management fees; however, as in other countries, fees are usually calculated on the basis of two parameters: either GAV or NAV.

GAV is the most commonly used fee basis for core and value added funds, while opportunity funds apply more varied fee bases. According to empirical analyses, it seems that Italian AMCs earning fees based on NAV are rather more cautious in leverage use and are more selective in their investment decisions.[6] Management fees calculated on the total assets seem to encourage leverage regardless of the quality of investment opportunities.

Asset management fees can be either fixed or variable:

- Fixed or base management fees are the costs of administering the fund and remunerate the AMC. They are calculated on a flat rate, based on the GAV or the NAV. According to the Regulation of the Bank of Italy of 19 January 2015, if fees are calculated on the GAV, eventual capital gains have to be excluded from the calculation.
- Variable management fees or performance/incentive/promote fees are performance related fees and can be calculated in several ways. Performance fees, or over-performance fees, are usually based on the achievement of a predefined target. They are widely used by investment managers, who typically charge a performance fee on

Table 3.4 Revenues and costs at each stage of a real estate fund.

Stage	Revenues	Costs
I **Fund start-up** Acquisition Contribution	-	Due diligence, advisory, legal Brokerage fees on acquisition (eventual) Bank interest and fees
	Revenues from properties	*Costs on properties*
II **Fund ordinary operation** Rent Development	Rents Other revenues (i.e temporary rents) Partial sales (eventual) Interest revenue (eventual)	Administration costs Italian property taxes Costs for vacant properties Registration taxes Insurance costs Brokerage fees on rents Maintenance Property management Facility management General contractor (for developments) Bank interest expense and fees Construction costs (eventual) Brokerage fees on sales/partial sales Banking/financing costs
III **Fund maturity** Divestment Liquidation	Sales	Brokerage fees on sales
		OTHER GENERAL COSTS ON FUND

Costs paid by the AMC		
Costs paid by the AMC Fund managers and advisors Asset management, eventual abort fees Legal, compliance, risk management Accounting, financing, cost to raise funds Internal head of valuation, analyses, research Administration, back office, investor relations	←	**Asset management company fees** **Auditor's report** **Independent valuer** **Depositary bank** **Asset management company performance fees**

Table 3.5 Fees by type of real estate fund.

Listed real estate funds	Non-listed real estate funds
Base fees from 0.70% to 1.80% on GAV.	Base fees from 0.40% to 1.80% on GAV.
Base fees from 0.90% to 1.90% on NAV.	Base fees from 0.50% to 2.80% on NAV.
Performance fees from 10% to 20% on the additional return over the target return, they do not differ whether Base fees are calculated on GAV or NAV.	Performance fees from 15% to 20% on the additional return over the target return.

The figures above are based on a general overview of the market and do not represent statutory limits or official market standards.

Table 3.6 Fees by type of initial contribution.

Capital contribution funds	Asset contribution funds
Base fees from 0.60% to 3.00% on GAV.	Base fees from 0.25% to 2.50% on GAV.
Base fees from 0.70% to 3.50% on NAV.	Base fees from 0.30% to 2.00% on NAV.
Performance fees from 10% to 20% on the additional return over the target return, they do not differ whether Base fees are calculated on GAV or NAV.	Performance fees from 15% to 30% on the additional return over the target return or different fees based on increase/decrease of assets under management.

The figures above are based on a general overview of the market and do not represent statutory limits or official market standards.

the results exceeding the target yield, as incentive fees based on the funds property return, or based on the increase in the GAV or NAV. Further variable management fees can be charged during the disinvestment period of the fund.

The performance fee may be charged in addition to the base management fee, therefore the total annual management fee of a fund is the sum of fixed and variable fees.

In addition to the above-mentioned fees, unitholders may be subject to:

- subscription fees, charged to a unitholder at the time of the initial investment in the fund;
- acquisition fees, which are an initial charge levied on the purchase of assets or initial fees related to a new portfolio acquisition (for capital contribution funds).

The amount of management fees depends on the:

- types of funds, i.e. listed vs. unlisted real estate funds;
- origin and structure of the assets, i.e. contribution funds based on an existing portfolio or pure investment funds based on new acquisitions;
- investment style, i.e. core, value-added, opportunistic;
- size of the portfolio under management.

With reference to the types of funds, fees related to listed real estate funds are generally higher compared to fees levied to non-listed real estate funds, partly due to the costs of the quotation process, to the stricter compliance procedure and to the detailed requirements of disclosure (Table 3.5).

Funds set up by total contribution of a portfolio of assets may require lower base management fees compared to funds established by partial contribution or to new real estate investment funds based on asset acquisitions yet to be made. This is due to the fact that investment funds have to raise initial capital and to analyse new investments while an already existing portfolio does not require the initial acquisition phase.

The minimum base management fees required by AMC are shown in Table 3.6. More in detail, in recent operations, involving portfolios previously directly owned and managed by a number of Italian welfare and assistance organisations, the minimum base management fees required by AMCs have been in the range of 0.35% and 0.4% of GAV.

The average management fee rate is nearly the same for core and value added funds, while it increases for opportunistic funds. The higher level of fees for non-core and opportunistic funds is due to their more time-consuming investment phase. Furthermore, performance fees have a major effect on the non-core funds and funds investing in development projects (Table 3.7).

Table 3.7 Fees by type of management strategy.

Core funds	*Value-added funds*	*Opportunistic funds*
Base fees from 0.40% to 1.80% on GAV.	Base fees from 0.50% to 2.00% on GAV.	Base fees from 0.60% to 3.50% on GAV.
Base fees from 0.50% to 1.90% on NAV.	Base fees from 0.70% to 2.80% on NAV.	Base fees from 0.80% to 3.80% on NAV.
Performance fees from 10% to 20% on the additional return over the target return.	Performance fees from 15% to 20% on the additional return over the target return.	Performance fees from 10% to 20% on the additional return over the target return; they do not differ whether Base fees are calculated on GAV or NAV.

The figures above are based on a general overview of the market and do not represent statutory limits or official market standards.

The range of fees described above often varies according to the size and number of properties under management.

Taxation

Contribution of assets

The contribution of properties to a real estate fund generates taxable income in the hands of the contributing entity. If the contributing entity is a company, the income/capital gain is subject to full corporate income taxation, with the possibility – in case the assets had been held for at least three years – to spread the taxable gain over a maximum of five tax periods. Any income can be offset with tax losses under ordinary rules.

Table 3.8 Taxable gain from the contribution of properties.

Taxable gain	=	Value of the fund units received by the contributing entity	−	Tax basis of the contributed properties

Table 3.9 Direct taxation on revenues due by the contributor of assets.

Transferor	IRES Corporate income tax	IRAP Regional tax on productive activities	Imposta sostitutiva Substitute tax
The property contributor is a **company** or an **entity subject to corporate tax.**	**27.5% on capital gain** The capital gain is computed as the difference between the contribution value of the asset and its relevant tax base, if the asset has been owned for more than 3 years; the tax can be paid in 5 yearly instalments. If there are losses carried forward, these would reduce the capital gain for IRES purposes to the extent allowed by ordinary rules.	**~3.9% on capital gain** The rate depends on the region where the asset is located and on the business sector.	**20% on capital gain** (including IRES and IRAP) by opting for the substitute tax regimen upon transfer. The application of the substitute tax is conditional upon the fund holding the asset for at least 3 years; the tax can be paid in 5 yearly instalments.

The formula explained in Table 3.8 determines the taxable income that may derive from the contribution of properties to a real estate fund.

A 20% substitute tax on taxable gain from contribution of properties to the fund applies under an optional regime (in this case, losses offset is not available). The 20% substitute tax applies alternatively to the ordinary tax regime, and may be paid entirely in one tax period or paid by instalments in up to five tax periods.

Assuming that the contributed assets are recorded within the fixed assets (not within current assets) of a company, the summary in Table 3.9 shows the direct taxes applicable to the contributing entity.

The contribution of an asset is regarded as a sale from a VAT point of view, while a contribution of a plurality of assets, mainly rented-out, is deemed as a supply of a going concern and as such outside the scope of VAT and being, instead, subject to registration, mortgage and cadastral taxes at 200 euro each. Therefore, the contribution of an asset is exempt from VAT, unless the asset is provided by the construction or refurbishment company within 5 years from completion or the transferor opts for applying VAT in the relevant deed. In this case, the VAT is due by the fund through the reverse charge mechanism, which is neutral for funds (Table 3.10).

Contribution of shares

A contribution of shares into a real estate fund impacts on the amount of revenue or of capital gains, depending on their recording in the financial statement of the transferor. The contribution to a fund of shares recognised in the financial statement as a fixed asset has an impact on capital gain or loss, instead if they are recognised as current assets their contribution raises revenues.

A capital gain or loss is equal to the difference between the fair value of the fund units received by the contributor and the adjusted tax basis of the contributed shares.

If a company contributes shares, 95% of the gain is exempt from IRES tax. However in order to obtain this exemption, it has to be provided that the company:

(i)   has recorded the shares as a fixed financial asset (long-term investment) in the first balance sheet of the holding period;
(ii) has continuously been holding the shares as of the first day of the 12th month preceding the disposal (for this purpose, the LIFO method applies);
(iii) is resident in Italy and has conducted a business activity in the three tax periods preceding the contribution (such condition is not regarded as met by real estate companies, other than real estate trading companies).

Table 3.10 Indirect taxation on the contribution of real assets.

Transferor	Cadastral registry category of the real asset	VAT regime	Other indirect taxes
1) VAT taxable entity (different from construction companies and entities carrying out building or refurbishment works)	I) Residential buildings	a) VAT exempt.	a) Registration Tax: 9% Mortgage Tax: € 50 – 200 Cadastral Tax: € 50 – 200
	II) Instrumental buildings	b) VAT exempt, unless the transferor exercises the option to apply VAT in the relevant deed.	b) Registration tax: € 200 Mortgage tax: **1.50%** Cadastral tax: **0.50%**
	III) Buildable lands	c) Subject to VAT.	c) Registration tax, Mortgage tax and Cadastral tax: € 200 each
2) Building companies or entities that have performed refurbishment works	I) Residential buildings	a) Subject to VAT if the transfer occurs within 5 years from the end of construction or refurbishment works. b) VAT exempt if the transfer occurs after 5 years from the end of construction or refurbishment works, unless the transferor exercises the option to apply VAT in the relevant deed.	a) Registration tax, Mortgage tax and Cadastral tax: € 200 each b) Registration tax: 9% Mortgage tax: € 50 – 200 Cadastral tax: € 50 – 200
	II) Instrumental buildings	a) Subject to VAT if the transfer occurs within 5 years from the date when the building or refurbishment works were finished or, if occurring afterwards, upon option exercised by the transferor in the transfer deed. b) VAT exempt if the transfer occurs after 5 years and provided that the transferor does not opt for the taxable regime.	a) Registration tax: € 200 Mortgage tax: **1.50%** Cadastral tax: **0.50%** b) Registration tax: € 200 Mortgage tax: **1.50%** Cadastral tax: **0.50%**
	III) Buildable lands	c) Subject to VAT.	c) Registration tax, Mortgage tax and Cadastral tax: € 200 each

Moreover the contributor may choose to spread realised capital gains in equal instalments over that year and the following ones, up to the fourth year. This option is only available in the case of disposal of assets that have been held for at least 3 years. The option is also available for assets that have been recorded as fixed financial assets in the financial statements of the last 3 years and that have not met the conditions for the access to the exemption regime seen above. The LIFO method applies for determining the holding period.

Finally, it is worth pointing out that the substitute tax of 20%, described above with reference to the contributions of assets to the fund, does not apply in this case.

The contribution of shares is an operation VAT exempt and subject only to registration tax at fixed amounts.

Taxation of funds and investors

Net income of real estate funds is tax exempt. In fact, in contrast with Italian companies, which are subject to IRES (the Corporate Income Tax) and

Table 3.11 Taxation at investor's level.

Italian-resident investors	Rates	Notes
No withholding tax is levied on dividends paid to: – Italian UCIs; – Italian pension funds; – assets under management under Article 7 of Legislative Decree no. 461 of 21 November 1997 (risparmio gestito); – SIIQs.	No withholding tax	Subject to taxation according to each specific regime
Individual entrepreneurs, companies and other entities, other than SIIQs, residing for tax purposes in Italy or permanent establishment in Italy of non-resident entities.	26%	Advance withholding tax (income is then subject to ordinary taxation with a credit for the paid withholding tax)
Individual unitholders (non-entrepreneurs).	26%	Final withholding tax
Non-resident investors	*Rates*	*Notes*
Companies and other entities.	26%	Final withholding tax
Individual unitholders.	26%	Final withholding tax
In case of applicability of double tax conventions, the applicable tax rate can be reduced.	Mainly at approx. 15%	

IRAP (the Regional Tax on Production), investment funds are pass through entities (soggetti lordisti).

Conversely, the profit of real estate funds is taxed only upon distribution, with the application of a withholding tax at investor's level, in proportion to his/her interest in the fund. With the same rationale, capital gains on fund units by investors are taxed according to the rules reported in Table 3.11.

Notes

1 Directive 2011/61/EU: Directive on AIFMs and amending Directives 2003/41/ EC and 2009/65/EC and Rules (EC) No 1060/2009 and (EU) No 1095/2010. Transposed in Italy by Legislative Decree no. 44 of 4 March 2014, Bank of Italy deed of 19 January 2015 and MEF Decree no. 30 of 5 March 2015.
2 Legislative Decree no. 58 of 24 February 1998. Article 1, subparagraph 1, provides the following definitions with regards to UCIs and AIFs:

> j) "investment fund": UCI constituted in the form of an enterprise with independent equity, divided into units, set up and managed by a fund manager;
> k) "undertaking for collective investment" (UCI): body set up to provide the service of the collective management of assets, the capital of which is obtained from multiple investors by the issue and offer of units or shares, managed upstream in the investors' interests and independently of the same and also invested in financial instruments, credit, including credit backed by the UCITS capital, equity or other fixed or non-fixed assets, on the basis of a predetermined investment policy;
> [...]
> k-ter) "closed-ended UCI": UCI other than open-ended UCIs;
> l) "Italian UCIs": investment funds, SICAVs and SICAFs;
> m-ter) "Italian alternative UCI" (Italian AIF): investment funds, SICAVs and SICAFs falling within the scope of application of Directive 2011/61/EU.

3 This principle is not affected by the presence of only one participant established as a stakeholder of a plurality by the law (i.e. a pension fund).
4 The Commissione Nazionale per le Società e la Borsa is the public authority responsible for regulating the Italian financial markets.
5 These AIFs have been introduced by art. 14bis of the Law no. 86 of 25th January 1994, amended by Law no. 410 of 23 November 2001, and by art. 13 of Decree of 5 March 2015 no. 30. The contribution shall include more than 51% of properties and/or rights contributed by the State, social security institutions, regions, local authorities or consortia as well as other companies wholly owned or indirectly owned by public entities.
6 Biasin and Quaranta (2012).

4 Real estate fixed capital investment companies (SICAFs)

Regulatory framework

The Legislative Decree no. 44 of 4 March 2014 has amended the TUF, establishing a new type of Italian undertaking for collective investment (UCI): the SICAF, i.e. investment company with fixed capital. More precisely, the SICAF is an investment scheme regulated as a closed-end UCI, set up as a limited company with fixed capital, subject to the rules of the AIFMD. As a consequence, the SICAF belongs to the category of the AIFs.

Therefore, the definition "investment company with fixed capital," within the meaning of the TUF, is: a company, the sole purpose of which is to invest its capital in stocks, properties or other assets with the single aim of diversifying risk and to provide a return for its shareholders thanks to the professional management of the assets. Listed SICAFs offer their own shares for underwriting by the public.

In addition, a SICAF is subject to part of the regulations of the Italian Civil code for joint-stock companies, i.e. the rights to the company capital and profits guaranteed by the shares as well as the regulation related to the shareholders' general meeting.

The SICAF regime is comparable to that applicable to Italian funds, except for the fact that the investment vehicle is set up with the form of a legal entity, i.e. a self-standing commercial company, instead of a segregated account within an asset management company, as described in the previous chapter about real estate funds.

Being a legal entity, the properties owned by the SICAF are registered under the name of the SICAF itself and not under the name of an asset management company on behalf of a fund. This regime allows for a clearer identification of the assets of the SICAF when compared to the real estate investment funds.

It is important to underline, moreover, that a SICAF can be set up in two different structures (Figure 4.1):

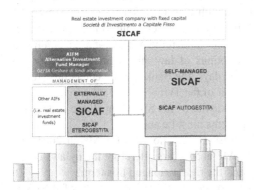

Figure 4.1 Self-managed and externally managed SICAFs.

- Self managed SICAF (SICAF autogestita). It is a SICAF having a board of directors composed of individuals that must meet the requirements set out by the Bank of Italy; it acts similarly to an asset management company investing directly (and not merely managing a fund) in alternative assets on a professional basis and with a greater operating flexibility compared to an AMC.
- Externally managed SICAF (SICAF eterogestita). It is a SICAF managed by an external AIFM.

Under the form of a joint stock company, the SICAF is responsible for its obligations with its own assets exclusively.

A SICAF, in compliance with the Italian TUF, must meet the following requirements:

- legal form of a company as a joint-stock company (i.e., società per azioni);
- registered office and headquarters of the company located in the Italian Republic;
- share capital amounts to at least the one determined as a general rule by the Bank of Italy;
- professionalism, integrity and independence of directors and managers, meeting criteria of competence and fairness and devoting the necessary time for the effective performance of their duties;
- ability to ensure the prudent management of the investee company for shareholders;
- structure of the group of which the company is part is not prejudicial to controls by the competent authorities and is not prejudicial to the effective supervision of the company.

Prior to the beginning of operations, the SICAF must be authorised by the Bank of Italy, in accordance with Consob, after an evaluation of the program with the initial activity, the report describing the organisational structure. The Bank of Italy also checks that the articles of association and bylaws comply with the prescriptions of law and regulations. After the authorisation, generally within 90 days, the Bank of Italy enters the SICAF in a register, according to art. 35ter of the TUF.

The company name must include the words SICAF in all the documents of the company. Financial statements must be audited.

According to art. 6 of the MEF Decree no. 30 of 5 March 2015, the maximum term of a real estate AIF is 50 years, therefore the bylaws of the SICAF establish the maturity and the right to extend this term.

The founders of the SICAF proceed to the establishment of the company and to making payments related to the start-up capital to be subscribed within 30 days from the date of the authorisation. The initial capital must be fully paid.

Shares of the SICAF represent a quota of participation in the company. Each shareholder is assigned a number of shares proportional to the capital subscribed, but the articles of association may provide a different assignment. Moreover, the articles of association must indicate the method for determining the value of the shares and of any participatory financial instrument issued.

The shares of the SICAF can be nominative or bearer, as established by the articles of association or by a subsequent amendment. Bearer shares attribute one vote to each shareholder, regardless of the number of shares held, and the articles of association may foresee the issue of shares without a right to vote or with limited or otherwise different rights to vote.

The shares entitle their owners to equal rights; however, the articles of association may establish classes of shares with different rights even with regard to the incidence of losses. In this case the company, in compliance with the limits established by law, can freely determine the rights of the shares of the various categories. All shares belonging to the same class confer equal rights. Each SICAF can issue an unlimited number of share classes, based on the needs of the specific clients to whom the shares can be sold.

SICAFs may issue fractional shares providing that the assignment and the exercise of rights are still subordinate to the possession of at least one share.

With reference only to reserved SICAFs, shareholders may subdivide the payments of the underwritten shares in instalments and pay their capital only upon request by the SICAF at the time of the acquisition of new assets.

SICAFs cannot issue bonds.

As for real estate funds, the contribution of assets, such as properties, is allowed.

SICAFs can be set up with a single investment portfolio (single compartment) or they can be structured as an umbrella (multi compartment) SICAF, which is divided into separate sub-segments (compartments) under the roof of a single legal entity. The articles of association establish the rights of the related shares. Each sub-segment has its own investment policy, target distribution market and investor profile. In the case of an umbrella SICAF, the assets of each compartment are segregated from those of the other ones.

In order to meet the information needs of investors, the SICAF is required to provide the following disclosure documents:

- financial statements;
- half-year reports on the management. This report is not required in the case of financial statements produced by the SICAF at least once every 6 months and related to the distribution of income;
- a schedule containing an indication of the unitary value of each share and the total value of the company, with periodicity at least equal to the issue or redemption of shares.

The same documents are required with reference to each compartment of the SICAF, if present.

The articles of association define the governing bodies and, if the SICAF is externally managed, provide for the appointment of an asset management company or an alternative investment manager charged of the management of the SICAF's assets.

Participants in a SICAF are both investors and shareholders and therefore can take part in the decision process related to the management of the assets. However, the managers of the SICAF can, in any case, ensure that the management of SICAF is done independently of the shareholders. Therefore, the actual powers of the shareholders should not be different from those of the unitholders for real estate investment funds. Unlike for funds, on the other hand, it is possible to modulate the governance of a SICAF with all the options already experimented with for Italian joint stock companies: voting lists, executive committees, diversified actions in rights, veto rights, rights and obligations of co-sale, etc.

Self-managed SICAFs are subject to controls and supervision with a structure similar to that of Italian AMCs, providing a full safeguard of investors' interests (Figure 4.2).

If the SICAF is externally managed, the articles of association must provide also for the instruction of the designated management company. The Bank of Italy may refuse the authorisation of an externally managed SICAF in cases where the technical or organisational situation of the designated management company does not ensure the ability of the latter to manage the assets of the SICAF in the interest of investors. The SICAF's assets are legally segregated from the assets of the external management company as well as from the assets of the other vehicles managed by the same management company.

Furthermore, externally managed SICAFs are subject to a complex structure of controls and supervision, but, given the presence of an asset management company (with AIFM status), in this regard they are more comparable to a real estate investment fund (Figure 4.3).

Figure 4.4 summarises the classification of real estate SICAFs, with types that have the same characteristics as those described with regards to the real estate investment funds.

Asset allocation and leverage

Similarly to real estate funds, SICAFs must allocate their assets for no less than two-thirds of the total in real estate, real estate rights (including those arising from real estate leases with translational nature) and investments in real estate companies and funds. This limit is reduced to 51% when at least 20% of the assets are invested into financial instruments deriving from the securitisation of real estate assets, property rights or receivables secured by real estate mortgages.

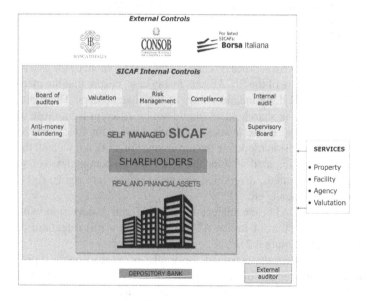

Figure 4.2 Structure of a self-managed real estate SICAF.

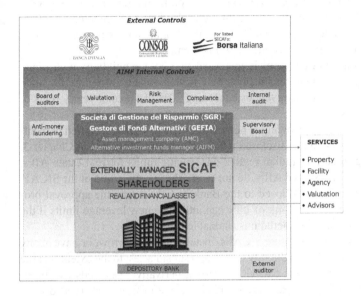

Figure 4.3 Structure of an externally managed real estate SICAF.

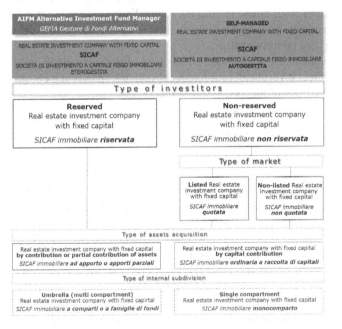

Figure 4.4 Types of real estate SICAFs.

With reference to concentration risk, a non-reserved real estate SICAF is not allowed to invest, directly or through subsidiaries, more than 20% of its assets in a single property with unitary use, zoning and characteristics, that can be considered marketable on a single unit basis.

This concentration limit is increased to 33% for buildings with rental purpose and the main tenant (including further tenants owned by the main tenant) produces rents/revenues exceeding 20% of the total yearly rents of the same asset.

Like any AIF, borrowing is permitted on the basis of a specified percentage of the asset value, disclosed within the bylaws. As stated in Chapter 3, according to current Italian regulation, specific limits for real estate AIFs, excluding non-reserved AIFs, do not exist. The leverage ratio of the SICAF, anyway, has to be disclosed to the Bank of Italy during the approval procedure, therefore the Bank of Italy can introduce new leverage limits if the original ones are considered unsustainable.

Non-reserved real estate SICAFs, instead, cannot borrow, or have at any given time borrowings directly or through subsidiaries, to the extent that the overall exposure of the SICAF (including derivatives) exceeds two times the NAV. In other words, the overall leverage of a non-reserved SICAF must be calculated as a ratio between the exposure of the SICAF and its NAV and must be lower than two. Real estate SICAFs must comply with the leverage limit at all times. In addition to this limit, real estate SICAFs are allowed to borrow temporarily within a limit of 10% of the NAV only in case of anticipated reimbursements.

Like real estate funds, SICAFs are not allowed to operate in direct building activity. Direct investment, or through subsidiaries, in building companies is limited at 10% of the total assets of the SICAF.

Main revenues, costs and fees

Real estate SICAFs and funds share the same business model and, therefore, the revenues and costs deriving from their properties can be regarded as coincident. For this reason, the reader may refer to Chapter 3 for further details.

With reference to the fees on SICAFs, it can be stated that shareholders of the externally managed SICAFs may be more proactive and the asset management company may charge lower management fees, especially if the SICAF is established by asset contribution.

Differently from a fund, the depositary bank does not calculate the value of the share. The SICAF has to calculate the participation values as well as all the values of the properties and of the assets owned in order to provide the NAV. As a consequence, the cost of this service may be marginally lower.

Table 4.1 Net fees subject to IRAP tax.

Subscription fees *Commissioni di sottoscrizione*	– Fees due to distributors *Commissioni passive dovute a soggetti collocatori*	= Net fees (Value of production) *Valore della produzione*

Nonetheless, these differences should not lead to significant disparities between the management and performance fees of a SICAF compared to the corresponding fees of a real estate fund.

Taxation

Article 9 of TUF extends to real estate SICAFs the same tax rules applicable to real estate investment funds, therefore tax rates due at the time of the contribution of real assets to a SICAF are in line with the ones described under Chapter 3 for real estate funds.

With reference to the possibility that an existing company applies for conversion into the SICAF regime, the current regulation does not provide for any substitute tax or entry tax. Therefore, if an existing company, ordinarily subject to corporate income tax (Imposta sul reddito delle società, IRES) and regional tax on productive activities (Imposta regionale sulle attività produttive, IRAP), applies for its conversion to the SICAF regime, it should be subject to IRES and IRAP on the gain deriving from the difference between the asset value reported in the financial statement of the former company and the new fair values of the SICAF.

On the contrary, the conversion of an existing real estate investment fund into a real estate SICAF is neutral for tax purposes.

The profit of a SICAF is taxed only upon distribution, with the application of a withholding tax at investor's level, as described in Chapter 3.

However, the above-mentioned article 9 of the TUF extends to SICAFs (regardless of the investment object, whether or not real estate assets) the provisions relating to IRAP tax on net commissions. The amount subject to IRAP tax is determined as reported in Table 4.1.

The law grants to SICAFs:

- a deduction of an amount equal to 90% of depreciation of tangible and intangible assets for operating purposes;
- a deduction of an amount equal to 90% of other administrative expenses.

The IRAP tax rate varies according to the Italian region in which the SICAF has its registered office.

5 Real estate investment trusts (SIIQs)

Regulatory framework

The Società di investimento immobiliare quotata (SIIQ) is an Italian listed real estate investment company similar to a REIT, subject to regulations introduced in Italy by the Law no. 296 of 27 December 2006 (art. 1, art. from 119 to 141), with subsequent amendments.

The SIIQ's main activity is the rental of real estate properties. According to the special tax regime applied to SIIQs, income deriving from rental activities is exempt from IRES and IRAP taxes, while other items of income are subject to the ordinary corporate and local taxation.

The company must be listed on a stock exchange in a recognised "White list" state.

The SIIQ regime is also applicable to a type of non-listed real estate investment company, named Società di investimento immobiliare non quotata (SIINQ), but only if it is a subsidiary of an SIIQ and if certain other conditions are met: its main activity is related to the lease of properties; it is controlled by an SIIQ with at least 95% of voting rights in the annual general meeting and in the profit-sharing, also in conjunction with other SIIQs; one of the above-mentioned controlling SIIQs satisfies the requirements for the consolidation of the SIINQ in order to adopt the group tax regime; its financial statements follow the International Financial Reporting Standards (IFRS).

As stated in art. 119-bis of the Law no. 296/2006, the SIIQ is not a closed-end real estate AIF and therefore it is not subject to the AIFMD.

SIIQs are under the supervision of Consob and, due to their special tax regime, they are overseen by the Agenzia delle Entrate, i.e. Italian Tax Agency (Figure 5.1). According to regulations, which are deliberately general, the Bank of Italy intervenes only when SIIQs interact with real estate funds. In all other cases, SIIQs remain subject to supervision by Consob, like any other listed company.

Figure 5.1 Structure of an SIIQ.

According to art. 1, a) of the Law Decree no. 174 of 7 September 2007, the SIIQ is a joint-stock company whose shares are listed on regulated markets, opting for the special tax regime and performing, according to the criteria of prevalence, the activities related to the rent of properties. The company is allowed to own the properties or to hold them under finance leases, as well as through other rights of use.

Income for special tax regime purposes may also derive from the development of property with a rental purpose or from shares in other SIIQs, SIINQs or in real estate AIFs specialised in rental of properties, representing long-term investments recorded within "financial fixed assets" (immobilizzazioni finanziarie), in accordance with the IAS/IFRS criteria.

In more detail, the special tax rules of the SIIQ regime may apply to companies:

- established as joint-stock companies (società per azioni);
- listing their shares on a recognised stock exchange ("White list" markets);
- residing, for tax purposes, in Italy (including foreign companies and entities having their administrative headquarters or their main activities in Italy for most of the tax period);
- residing, for tax purposes, in the European Union and "White list" countries;
- having a permanent establishment in Italy;
- carrying out property rental activities;
- including the acronym SIIQ as part of the company's name.

The bylaws (statuto) of the SIIQ must define:

- the investment rules adopted by the company;
- the limits established in order to prevent risks of investment concentration and counterparty risk related to contractual obligations and default risk;
- the limits to leverage on an individual and group basis.

With regards to the shareholder structure, the special SIIQ tax regime is applicable only if the following restrictions, known as "requisito del controllo," are met (Figure 5.2):

- a single shareholder does not hold, directly or indirectly, more than 60% of the voting rights and is not entitled to more than 60% of the profit rights;
- at the date of election of the SIIQ regime, at least 25% of SIIQ's shares must be held by shareholders not holding, directly or indirectly, 2% or more of the voting rights or 2% or more of dividend rights.

The 25% requirement is not applicable to companies already listed.

Similarly, Borsa Italiana requires at least 25% free float (portion of shares in the hands of public investors) for IPOs. This requirement includes the shares pledged with voting and profits rights on behalf of the creditor.

The main activity of the SIIQ must be the business of property rental. All income deriving from renting activities executed directly, or through

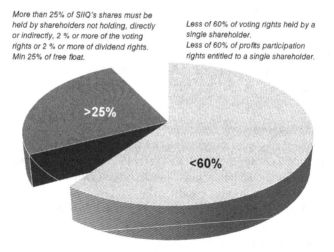

Figure 5.2 Shareholder structure and restrictions.

subsidiaries and participations in other similar vehicles (i.e., other SIIQs, SIINQs, real estate AIFs specialised in renting activity), will be part of the tax exempt business (gestione esente). The renting activity may be related to all uses and types of buildings or developments/refurbishments (including social housing), owned directly by the SIIQ or under a right of use (i.e. financial leasing or usufruct). Income can derive from rent agreements, from business leases (affitto di ramo d'azienda) or other forms of contract (i.e. right of use).

On the contrary, there are no specific restrictions regarding the activities that may be carried out by SIIQ or SIINQ under the ordinary tax regime. Every other business, however, must be described in the bylaws of the company.

Table 5.1 provides a summary of the tax exempt and taxable business.

A company, in order to be granted the tax regime of SIIQ, must pass the asset test, i.e. at least 80% of the total value of the assets must be intended for the renting activity, as explained in Table 5.2.

Another requisite for the SIIQ tax regime, known as profit or income test, is that at least 80% of the total revenues of the company must be generated from the renting activity (in each tax period), including income distributions from other SIIQs, SIINQs, real estate AIFs and SICAFs or from non-listed Italian companies carrying out a renting activity (Table 5.3).

The application to the special SIIQ tax regime must be made providing a written notice to the Italian Tax Agency (Agenzia delle Entrate) before the beginning of the tax period in which the regime should start. The SIIQ tax regime starts from the first tax year after the acceptance of the application.

Furthermore the company must be listed on the stock exchange of a "White list" state. An admission application must be submitted to Borsa Italiana pursuant to the "Rules of the markets organised and managed by

Table 5.1 Tax exempt and taxable business.

Tax exempt business	Taxable business
Rental activity of properties owned as freehold or by another right of use (financial lease, usufruct or other real right).	Income from other activities, i.e. from facility management, technical assistance, trading, consultancy, etc.
Development/refurbishment of properties for rental purpose.	
Maintenance of building for rental purpose.	
Investment in shares of other SIIQs, SIINQs and real estate AIFs investing at least 80% of assets in properties with a renting purpose.	

Table 5.2 Asset test.

ASSET TEST =	Total value of the assets for renting purposes + total value of participations accounted as fixed assets in SIIQs, SIINQs and real estate AIFs investing 80% in ≥ 80% rented properties or investments in real estate companies such as SIIQs or SIINQs ("Qualified RE AIFs") ――――――――― TOTAL ASSET VALUE *(Attivo di Stato Patrimoniale)*	Including: • properties under development/refurbishment; • participations in other SIIQs or SIINQs held for investment purposes. Excluding: • head office or other offices directly occupied and used by the SIIQ; • liquidity not yet invested; • intra-group loans; • not collected receivables and VAT credit of the tax exempt business; • derivates; • tax credits; • prepayments.

Table 5.3 Profit test.

PROFIT TEST =	Proceeds from rental activity + part of dividends deriving from rents distributed ≥ 80% by participations in other SIIQs, SIINQs, qualified real estate AIFs ――――――――― TOTAL REVENUES *(Componenti positivi del Conto economico)* Total revenues excluding: • cost adjustments; • contingent gains; • deferred taxes; • cost-sharing arrangements; • insurance reimbursements; • non-effective instalments of interest rate swaps; • positive components from obligations.	Including: • capital gains from sales of properties for letting purposes; • capital gains from sales of participations and shares. Excluding: • profits from dividends not related to rental activity or from reserves; • gains from progress of works in developments for lease purpose; • increase of the fair values due to periodical valuations and other increases in the book inventories.

Borsa Italiana." The publication of a prospectus approved by Consob is required in order to apply to regulated markets in Italy. In the case of foreign companies from the European Union, the prospectus must be approved by the competent home Authority, pursuant to the "home country control" rule.

Following the admission decision by Borsa Italiana, the procedure will be completed when Borsa Italiana, after ascertaining that the prospectus has been made available to the public, establishes the date for the beginning of trading.

Existing SIIQs are traded on MTA (Mercato Telematico Azionario – Italian Equities Market), the main market dedicated to medium and large cap companies and in line with best international standards, as well as on AIM Italia (Alternative Investment Market), the market of Borsa Italiana devoted to the Italian small and medium enterprises, which wish to invest in their growth. Instead, the SIIQs that have not yet invested the capital raised must be listed on the professional segment of the MIV market.

Due to the SIIQ's legal form as a company limited by shares, the capital of SIIQ may be composed of registered shares or bearer shares. The shares must be of equal value and entitle their owners to equal rights. However, the articles of association may create shares with different rights. The articles of association define the methods for determining the value of shares and of any other equity financial instruments issued. Generally no reimbursements of shares are foreseen in the articles of association.

The mandatory form of joint-stock company of the SIIQ ensures clear segregation of the assets of the SIIQ from any other assets of third parties, including shareholders. Assets are directly owned by the SIIQ itself and are registered under the name of the SIIQ.

The SIIQ is organised following the same model of corporate governance used for the Italian joint-stock companies. Therefore, the SIIQ is self-managed, as there is no obligation of external management.

According to Law Decree no. 133 of 12 September 2014, which amended art. 1, subparagraph 123 of Law no. 296 of 27 December 2006, the application of the SIIQ tax regime is subject to the obligation of distributing income on a yearly basis (Table 5.4).

The requirement of distributing profits from the tax exempt business is influenced by eventual losses derived from the taxable business. Assuming a loss in taxable business of 30 million euro, the total net income shall decrease by 30 million as well as the related distribution obligation of the period. However, according to a carry-forward methodology, the loss that has contracted the distribution obligation shall be taken into account in the following years in order to increase by 30 million the bases for the distribution obligations as soon as profits become available (see the example in Table 5.5).

Similarly, a loss in the tax-exempt business, which erases the yearly distribution obligation, can be carried forward, increasing the net income subject to distribution obligation of the following year. However, eventual profit distribution exceeding the obligation amount cannot be considered

Table 5.4 Income distribution.

	Types of income	Minimum % of yearly distribution
Tax-exempt business	The lower amount between total profits and net profits deriving from: • real estate rental income; • income from participations in other SIIQs or SIINQs; • income from shares in reserved real estate AIFs and SICAFs.	70
	The lower amount between total profit and net profit deriving from: • income from sales of properties with renting purpose; • income from sales of participations in other SIIQs or SIINQs; • income from sales of shares in reserved real estate AIFs and SICAFs.	50
Taxable business	Activities other than rental (e.g. consultancy, sale of other products, etc.).	Not subject to yearly distribution

an anticipation of future profit distributions according to the carry-forward methodology, as there are no limits related to the over-distribution exceeding the 70% and 50% rates.

The minimum distribution obligation of 70% or 50% of net profits is established and decided upon the approval of the financial statements at the end of the yearly financial period, independently of any other distributions approved on other dates. Therefore, extraordinary distributions or other reserve distributions decided in other periods are excluded.

Capital gains derived from the increase in the value of properties, calculated on a yearly basis in compliance with IAS 40, should be allocated within a reserve unavailable for distribution (riserva indisponibile), that may decrease according to possible depreciations or after sales, if capital gains have been achieved.

According to the recapture rule, the distribution obligation on capital gains derived from sales must take into account the amount calculated in the asset valuations during the previous years.

Even if not subject to distribution obligation, income deriving from the activities excluded by the special tax regime should be detailed in the financial statements.

Table 5.5 Example of distribution obligation.

Assuming that the SIIQ is at its 4th year of special tax regime	Year X + 4		Year X + 5		Year X + 6		Year X + 7		Year X + 8		Year X + 9	
Net income description	%	Mln €	%	Mln €	%	Mln €	%	Mln €	%	Mln €	%	Mln €
Total net income from tax exempt business (T.E.B. at 70% + c.g., T.E.B. at 50%)		**160**		**150**		**130**		**70**		**−10**		**110**
Net income from taxable business (T.B.)		20		−30		20		30		60		50
Total net income T.E.B. + T.B.		**180**		**120**		**150**		**100**		**50**		**160**
Decrease due to net losses, Increase due to absorbable losses				−30		20		10		−10		10
Outstanding losses to be absorbed				*30*		*10*		*0*		*10*		*0*
T.E.B. (including decrease or increase)	100	**160**	100	**120**	100	**150**	100	**80**	100	**0**	100	**120**
T.E.B. at 70% net income from tax exempt business from renting (proportion)	100	**160**	50	**60**	60	**90**	100	**80**	70	0	100	**120**
c.g. T.E.B. at 50% within 3Y / Net income from capital gain (proportion)	0	0	50	60	40	60	0	0	30	0	0	0
Distribution obligation on T.E.B. at 70%												
T.E.B. at 70% net income from tax exempt business from renting (proportion)	100	**160**	50	**60**	60	**90**	100	**80**	70	0	100	**120**
Distribution obligation of T.E.B. at 70%	70	**112**	70	**42**	70	**63**	70	**56**	70	**0**	70	**84**
Distribution obligation on c.g. T.E.B. at 50%												
c.g. T.E.B. at 50% within 3Y / Net income from capital gain (proportion)	0	**0**	50	60	40	60	0	0	30	0	0	0
Distr. obligation c.g. T.E.B. at 50% within 3Y	50	0	50	30	50	30	50	0	50	0	50	0
T.E.B. at 50% postponed (max 2Y)		*0*	*60*	*−18*	*100*	*−30*		*0*		*0*		*0*
T.E.B. at 50% to be distributed		**0**	40	**12**		**18**	50	**15**		**0**	50	**0**
T.E.B. at 50% postponed or cumulated				*18*		*30*		*15*		*15*		
Distribution T.E.B. at 50% deliberated		**0**		**12**		**18**		**15**		**15**		**0**
Total distribution T.E.B. at 70% obligation + c.g. T.E.B. at 50% deliberated		**112**		**54**		**81**		**71**		**15**		**84**

All the requirements for access to the special tax regime have to be maintained over time. However, the law permits a so-called "grace period" of three consecutive financial years, during which the SIIQ is allowed to fail to fulfil one of the requirements, not necessarily the same in each year, for its special tax regime. On the other hand, starting from the second year of the unfulfilled requirements, i.e. at the beginning of the third year, the ordinary Italian tax regime has to be applied.

The special SIIQ tax regime can be terminated by the Agenzia delle Entrate in the cases described in Table 5.6. The free float percentage limit is only an initial requirement, but not a termination matter, as the float percentage is a variable that cannot be kept under control by the SIIQ. No penalties are provided in case of withdrawal of the SIIQ status.

Asset allocation and leverage

The regulations related to SIIQs have not set specific limits on investments, excluding the above-mentioned rules requiring that at least 80% of the total value of the assets must be held for renting purposes.

With reference to investment timing, new SIIQs must invest at least 50% of their assets by the date of the beginning of activity, in compliance with the rules stated by the Stock Exchange concerning the MIV market. According to the rules stated by Borsa Italiana relating to the MIV, the investment policy of the SIIQ is required to comply with the following rules: at least three investments, none of

Table 5.6 Causes of termination of the SIIQ tax regime.

Causes of loss of the SIIQ status	Consequences
Asset test < 80% and/or Profit test < 80%	Allowed for at least 3 consecutive years (grace period), but ordinary tax regime starting from the 2nd year in which the SIIQ does not meet the asset and/or profit test.
Failure to distribute at least 70% of the total net profit from renting activity. Failure to distribute at least 50% of the total net profit from capital gain.	End of the special tax regime during the year in which the distribution obligation is unfulfilled.
Loss of the joint-stock company form.	End of the special tax regime during the year of loss of the joint-stock company form.
Revocation of the listing on a stock exchange.	End of the special tax regime during the year of revocation.
Presence of a shareholder exceeding the threshold of 60%. Loss of shareholder requirements (except for the 2% requirement).	End of the special tax regime during the year of loss of shareholder requirements.

which represents more than 50% of the total assets of the company, and at least three tenants, none of which represents more than 50% of the rental income.

No limits to leverage are set up by existing regulations and therefore the SIIQ can determine its own leverage limit, but the bylaws must establish the maximum leverage ratio allowed.

Direct construction activity is allowed as well as the acquisition of shares of construction companies, within the rental purpose investment limits. These activities are part of taxable business, if not related to rental business.

Main revenues and costs

Table 5.7 summarises the main revenues and costs of a typical SIIQ, with its business focusing on the renting of properties. More details about rents in the Italian space market are available in Table 3.2.

Table 5.7 Main revenues and costs of rented properties of SIIQs.

Income	
Gross rental income	See Table 3.1.
Asset related operating expenses	
Registration tax	Between 0.5% and 2% of the total amount of the rents, referred to the whole lease period. Fixed amount of 200 € in the case of financial lease of buildings.
Stamp duty	Not significant (16 € every four written pages of the contract).
VAT on rents	Renting agreements signed by SIIQs fall within the scope of VAT.
Other expenses	
Brokerage fees on new rent contracts	Approximately 10% of first annual rent.
Insurance	Insurance premiums, depending on the building replacement costs and on the yearly amount of potential rent loss.
Property taxes	The main municipal taxes related to properties have been encased under the single definition of IUC, which is composed of the three tax rates: IMU, TASI, TARI. Different coefficients are provided by law according to the different types of property.
Property management fees	Between 0.80% and 2.5% of annual rents for tenants management plus a mark up on maintenance costs for the facility management services.

(continued)

Table 5.7 (continued)

Other expenses

Non-recoverable service charges + contingency + other	Service charges not covered by the tenant, costs for vacant units, legal fees, etc.
	May include all the costs normally charged to the tenants, i.e. fixed and common expenses for the properties located within condominiums. Accounting and administration fees, aborted purchase costs, etc.
Capex or maintenance	Depending on age and state of repair of the buildings.
VAT on expenses	The taxable entity subject to VAT is the SIIQ itself.

TOTAL asset related operating expenses

Net rental income	Gross rental income less total asset related operating expenses.

Other revenue

Net income from services	Services as facility management, technical assistance, trading, consultancy, etc. subject to ordinary taxation regime.

Other operating expenses

Cost of employees	All the employer costs for wages, salaries, employee benefits, etc.
General costs	Other costs, i.e. contingencies, external advisory fees, legal fees, etc.

Total operating expenses

Other costs	Advisory costs, administrative costs, etc.
Incomes from asset sales (buildings for trading purposes)	Buildings included in the portfolio that have been classified for trading purposes on the basis of their use, quality, size, vacancy status, etc.
Gains(/losses) from asset sales (buildings for trading purposes)	Revenues from asset sales minus cost of sold assets.
Costs on sales	Real estate agent's fees (between 2% and 3% plus VAT, depending on size, use, type of market, etc.). Costs of mortgage cancellation if the property is subject to a mortgage. Other costs, e.g. marketing, advertising, etc.
Net financial income	Bank interest and fees.
Gains(/losses) from subsidiaries and associates	Gains or losses from participation in other companies.
Taxation	Taxes on income from taxable business.

Net income

In addition to traditional financial ratios and margins, the financial statement analysis of SIIQs makes use of a measure known as funds from operations (FFO). It is a multiple approach to valuing REITs throughout the world and is regarded as the industry standard in determining REITs profitability for shareholders. FFO adjusts for gains (or losses) on the sale of properties, because they are not recurring and therefore do not contribute to the SIIQ's ongoing dividend-paying capacity.

The adjusted funds from operations (AFFO), moreover, modifies the FFO taking into account rent increases and certain capital expenditures.

Table 5.8 provides the detailed calculation of the FFO and AFFO.

Taxation

SIIQ tax regime

The SIIQ tax regime is unique in the system of Italian taxation and, therefore, it requires an in-depth examination.

An entry tax of 20% on capital gains can be applied to the contribution to an SIIQ of properties eligible for the tax-exempt business. Entry tax is applied as explained in Table 5.9.

Companies applying for the conversion into an SIIQ or SIINQ benefit from the opportunity of increasing their real estate assets taxable value, as the fair value mentioned above will be the new taxable value. The new established taxable value will be effective as of the fourth year following the application of the special tax regime (1 year before the start of the regime for the application plus 3 years from the start of the special tax regime). Furthermore, fair value (valore normale) will become the basis of the asset test.

Table 5.8 Calculation of FFO and AFFO.

Net income (Earnings before taxes)	
Real estate depreciation	+
Gain on property sales	−
Other misc. depreciation items and gains	+
= FFO Funds from Operations	=
Capital expenditures	−
Other amortisation	−
= AFFO Adjusted Funds from Operations	=

Table 5.9 Entry substitute tax.

Fair value	–	**Taxable value**	=	**Capital gains**
Valore normale, valore equo		*Costo fiscalmente riconosciuto*		Subject to **20%** entry tax
The price that would be received in exchange of an asset or paid to transfer a liability in an orderly transaction between market participants at the measurement date, net of directly attributable expenses.		The amount attributed to the asset or liability for tax purposes before the special tax exempt regime (i.e. including purchase cost, notary's fees, capitalised costs and any subsequent additions, and net of depreciation and amortisation).		

Table 5.10 Ordinary tax on capital gains.

Fair value	–	**Taxable value = Capital gains**	Subject to **ordinary taxation**
Already used to calculate the 20% entry tax.		Before special regime, net of the amortisation.	

A favourable 20% substitute tax is payable by companies in five equal annual instalments (plus interest). This option can also be applied to properties intended for sale (i.e. taxable businesses). Alternatively, capital gains can be taxed in the ordinary regime or can be included within the taxable business of the company before the special tax regime.

Tax losses incurred during pre-conversion tax periods can be carried forward and can be offset against capital gains subject to the entry substitute tax or against the taxable income.

The entry tax regime can be applied also to properties held to be sold, provided that their intended use is changed and therefore their recording in the financial statement is changed from current assets to fixed assets.

If the assets are sold before the 3rd fiscal year since the application to the special tax regime or the company does not meet the requirements, capital gains are subject to ordinary tax, as shown in Table 5.10.

However, the 20% entry tax already paid by the future SIIQ on the above-mentioned anticipated sales can be recovered as tax credit, decreasing the future corporate income tax. After the sale of a property, the eventual capital gain to be inserted in the tax-exempt business of the SIIQ is the result of sale price less the above-mentioned fair value.

Similarly, in cases where the SIIQ does not comply with all the requirements of the special tax regime, it will be subject to ordinary taxation at the time of tax reviews (ex post).

Following the innovations introduced by the Law Decree no. 133 of 12 September 2014, amending Law no. 296 of 27 December 2006, the investment in a real estate AIF can be converted into an investment in an SIIQ in a tax-neutral way. In this case, the real estate AIF, contributing all or part of its assets, assigns to its unitholders/shareholders a proportional amount of shares of an SIIQ. Usually this procedure is followed when the SIIQ is already in existence.

With regards to the taxation on the SIIQ, income deriving from property renting is exempt from the corporate income tax (Imposta sul reditto delle società, IRES) and from the regional tax on productive activities (Imposta regionale sulle attività produttive, IRAP), starting from the tax exempt period.

Income arising from other businesses (i.e. taxable business) is subject to taxation under ordinary rules and therefore is subject to the corporate income tax and the regional tax on productive activities. The SIIQ must calculate the result of the taxable business in addition to the tax-exempt amount. Any losses deriving from tax-exempt business cannot offset taxable income.

Capital gains deriving from the disposal of rented real estate properties and investments in SIIQs, SIINQs or qualifying real estate AIFs are tax exempt, as well as proceeds from rents distributed by qualifying real estate AIFs.

Taxation of investors

Focusing on the taxation of investors in SIIQs, it is necessary to subdivide dividends on the basis of their sources: arising from the tax exempt business profits and arising from the taxable business profits.

With regards to the tax exempt business, the rates of the withholding tax applied on dividends distributed to the different categories of shareholders resident in Italy are reported in Table 5.11. The withholding tax is levied by the custodian of the SIIQ shares, i.e. an Italian bank or investment company.

The tax regime of dividends from the tax exempt business distributed to non-resident investors is shown in Table 5.12.

Dividends derived from profits of the taxable business are subject to ordinary taxation for Italian-resident corporate taxpayers, but eligible for a 95% exclusion from taxation.

For non-resident investors, pursuant to certain conditions, according to the Parent-Subsidiary Directive[1] the dividends distributed by a subsidiary

Table 5.11 Dividends from tax exempt business to Italian-resident shareholders.

Italian-resident investors	Rates	Notes
• Other SIIQs. • Italian undertakings for collective investment. • Italian pension funds. • Assets under management under Article 7 of Legislative Decree no. 461 of 21 November 1997 (risparmio gestito).	**No withholding tax**	Subject to taxation according to each specific regime
Individual entrepreneurs, companies and other entities, other than SIIQs, residing for tax purposes in Italy or permanent establishment in Italy of non-resident entities.	26%	Advance withholding tax (income is then subject to ordinary taxation with a credit for the paid withholding tax)
Individual shareholders (non-entrepreneurs) holding a "non-substantial" participation (i.e. not representing more than 2% of the voting rights or 5% of the capital). Dividends derived from exempted distributed earnings will be subject to a final 26% withholding tax when distributed.	26%	Final withholding tax
Individual shareholders (non-entrepreneurs) holding a "substantial" participation (i.e. representing more than 2% of the voting rights or 5% of the capital). Dividends are included in the taxable income subject to progressive taxation to the extent of 49.72% of their amount.	**No withholding tax**	Personal income tax at progressive rates

Table 5.12 Dividends from tax exempt business to non-resident shareholders.

Non-resident investors	Rates	Notes
Companies and other entities.	26%	Final withholding tax
Individual shareholders.	26%	Final withholding tax
In case of applicability of double tax conventions, the applicable tax rate can be reduced.	Mainly at approx. **15%**	

to an EU holding company are exempt from taxes. The Parent-Subsidiary Directive is applicable to the portion of non-exempt dividends deriving from taxable business. In other cases, the dividends paid to non-resident corporate shareholders are subject to a withholding tax at the following rates:

- 1.375% in case the beneficial owner is a company resident in a EU/EEA member state, subject to corporate income tax in its state of residence;
- 26% in all other cases, subject to possible reduction under applicable double tax conventions.

Dividends paid to non-resident individuals out of non-exempt income are subject to the ordinary applicable taxation, with possible reduction under applicable double tax conventions.

A final detail about the tax regime of SIIQ regards the capital gains from the sale of SIIQ shares. For Italian-resident corporate taxpayers, the capital gains resulting from the disposal of SIIQ shares is fully subject to corporate income taxes at regular rates. For Italian-resident non-business taxpayers, if the sold SIIQ shareholding represents a substantial participation (i.e. more than 2% of the voting rights or 5% of the capital), capital gains are subject to full taxation. Conversely, if the SIIQ shareholding does not represent a substantial participation, capital gains realised by Italian resident individuals are subject to a 26% capital gains tax.

For non-resident shareholders, capital gains arising from the sale of shares in SIIQs are subject to the tax regime ordinarily applicable to Italian shares, including specific domestic and treaty exemptions available to non-residents. Exemptions may be available for non-resident individuals or companies, without a permanent establishment, under double taxation treaties, to be verified on a case by case basis.

Note

1 Directive 2003/123/EC.

6 Italian AIFs and SIIQs

Comparative analysis

Real estate investment funds vs. SICAFs

Taking into account the main differences described in the preceding chapters between real estate funds, SICAFs and SIIQs, this convenience analysis is carried out by comparing the categories of vehicles that are similar and that may be regarded as alternatives from the point of view of a rational investor.

A first comparison can be drawn between real estate investment funds and SICAFs, because these instruments share the same legal nature of UCIs of the category of AIF.

Table 6.1 summarises the main points of convergence and divergence between these two types of AIFs. The symbols identify the presence of a clear advantage or disadvantage for the investor in choosing one of the two categories of instruments.

Leaving aside the cases in which no specific model of AIF shows prevalence, it can be noticed that, first of all, self-managed SICAFs do not require the presence of an external manager, i.e. a Società di gestione del risparmio (SGR) or asset management company (AMC). This aspect, due to the fact that SICAFs, unlike funds, are legal entities, is the source of several differences between these two AIFs.

The governance of SICAFs is very simplified, with a clear power of shareholders in the appointment of managers. On the other hand, these managers have a degree of freedom in the definition of the investment policies which is somewhat higher than in funds, due to the necessary involvement of the unitholder assembly in this latter AIF.

Another advantage of the SICAFs if compared to the real estate funds is the right of the former to be the direct owner of the assets of their portfolio. The assets of funds, instead, must be placed under the ownership of the asset management company. This type of ownership is less clear than the direct one, especially for non-Italian investors who are not accustomed to this trilateral structure.

Table 6.1 Comparison of real estate funds and SICAFs.

	Real estate funds	Real estate SICAFs
Structure	Trilateral structure: Asset management company + real estate fund + assets. Legal structure based on a contract between the asset management company and investors.	If externally managed, trilateral structure: management company + real estate SICAF + assets. Legal structure of a company with a contract with an asset management company. If self-managed, bilateral structure: management + assets. More flexible. Legal structure of a company.
Ownership	No restrictions, even though a plurality of investors is required. For listed funds: min. 25% free float (Borsa Italiana stock exchange rule for admission on the MIV market).	No restrictions, even though a plurality of investors is required. For listed SICAFs: min. 25% free float (Borsa Italiana stock exchange rule for admission on the MIV market).
Authorisation	Not subject to specific authorisation, the asset management company must comply with all the requirements.	Authorisation by the Bank of Italy in consultation with Consob.
Fund rules/articles of association	Defined by the asset management company.	Authorised by the Bank of Italy.
Governance	Governance of the asset management company selected by the unitholders.	Direct appointment of the managers by the SICAF shareholders.
Subscription	Funds units.	Registered shares or bearer shares.
Reimbursements	At liquidation, partial or anticipated reimbursements allowed only if stated by fund rules.	At liquidation, partial or anticipated reimbursements allowed only if stated by the articles of association.
Investment limits	> 2/3 (66.67%) real estate assets; > 51% real estate assets, when at least 20% of the assets are invested into financial instruments.	> 2/3 (66.67%) real estate assets; > 51% real estate assets, when at least 20% of the assets are invested into financial instruments.
Investment policies	Changes to investment policies normally require some form of investors' consent.	Investment policies may be changed at the board's discretion.
Segregation of assets	Assets owned by the asset management company on behalf of the fund.	Assets directly owned by the SICAF, even if externally managed.

Listed real estate AIFs vs. SIIQs

One of the main advantages of the investment vehicles of financial real estate, compared to the direct ownership of properties, is their liquidity, especially for listed instruments. It is useful, therefore, to focus on the Italian financial instruments available to investors interested in the real estate asset class and, at the same time, with a strong liquidity preference.

The regulation on the ownership composition of SIIQs is more articulated than the one affecting listed real estate AIFs, i.e. real estate funds and SICAFs, but it should be noted that SIIQs are more oriented towards retail investors than AIFs.

The governance of SIIQs, on the other hand, is more clear and simple than the one of externally managed AIFs, while self-managed SICAFs share with SIIQs a similar degree and kind of control of shareholders over the management.

Again, the SIIQs and SICAFs, both legal entities, are the sole and direct owners of their real and financial assets, while an asset management company is required as legal owner of the assets of a real estate fund.

The profiles of cash flows distributed to investors are quite different between listed AIFs and SIIQs. While the former investment vehicles can distribute their profits and the revenues of their sales according to their own policies, SIIQs are subject to a compulsory distribution of income, providing steadier cash flows to its shareholders but also a lower degree of discretionality to its managers. On the other hand, no limits are imposed by regulators on the leverage of SIIQs, while listed AIFs must comply with the constraints calculated according to the methodology defined by the EU Commission Delegated Regulation no. 231/2013.

SIIQs can operate directly in the building activity, unlike AIFs, but this business is outside of the perimeter of tax exemption. SIIQs, therefore, can benefit from a higher degree of freedom of business, but this advantage is partially counterbalanced by the absence of a special tax regime.

The open-end nature of SIIQs, moreover, can limit the risk of a sale off of assets during the liquidation phase, typical of closed-end instruments such as real estate AIFs. On the other hand, owners of units/shares of listed real estate funds or SICAFs can liquidate their investment both on the market and at the final liquidation of the AIF, while this latter option is not present for the shareholders of SIIQs.

As a concluding remark, SIIQs and SICAFs, these latter especially if self-managed, offer a simple and useful instrument for investment in the Italian real estate. Funds, on the other hand, constitute the most mature and developed instrument present on the Italian market and, therefore, allow investors a wider degree of choice and diversification, but offer no other

Table 6.2 Comparison of listed real estate AIFs and SIIQs.

	Listed real estate AIFs (funds and SICAFs)	SIIQs
Structure	Funds and externally managed SICAFs. Trilateral structure: management + real estate AIF + assets. Self-managed SICAFs. Bilateral structure: management + assets.	Bilateral structure: management + assets
Ownership	No restrictions, even though a plurality of investors is required. Min. 25% free float (Borsa Italiana stock exchange rules for admission to the MIV market).	More than 25% of SIIQ's shares must be held by shareholders not holding, directly or indirectly, 2% or more of the voting rights or 2% or more of dividend rights. Min. 25% free float (Borsa Italiana stock exchange rules for admission to the MTA and MIV markets). Less than 60% voting rights held by a single shareholder. Less than 60% profits participation rights due to a single shareholder.
Authorisation	Funds: not subject to specific authorisation, but the AMC must comply with all the requirements. SICAFs: authorisation from the Bank of Italy in consultation with Consob. Listed Funds/SICAF: admission application to Borsa Italiana stock exchange.	Admission application to Borsa Italiana stock exchange.
Governance	Funds and externally managed SICAFs: asset management company selected by the unitholders/shareholders. Self-managed SICAFs: direct appointment of directors by the shareholders.	Direct appointment of directors by the shareholders.
Investment limits	> 2/3 (66.67%) real assets. > 51% real assets when at least 20% of the assets are allocated to financial real estate instruments.	Profit test and asset test.

(continued)

Table 6.2 (continued)

	Listed real estate AIFs (funds and SICAFs)	SIIQs
Investment policies	Funds: changes to investment policies normally require some form of investors' consent. SICAFs: investment policies may be changed at the board's discretion.	Investment policies, subject to board's discretion.
Segregation of assets	Funds: assets owned by the AMC on behalf of the fund. SICAFs: assets directly owned.	Assets directly owned by the SIIQ.
Reimbursements, distribution	Upon liquidation, partial or anticipated reimbursements admitted.	Yearly distribution of profits from the tax exempt business.
Leverage	Non-reserved AIFs are subject to limits to leverage.	No compulsory limit of leverage.
Building activity	Direct construction activity not allowed; investments in construction companies limited to 10% of the total assets.	Direct construction activity allowed; investments in construction companies not limited. Both belong to the taxable business.
Maturity	Pre-defined maturity, often contingent on the investment goals or status of individual investors.	No fixed maturity.
Costs	Funds and externally managed SICAFs: costs of external manager (asset management company). Self-managed SICAFs: costs similar to those of an asset management company.	Cost of the internal management.
Taxation at vehicle level	Exempt, but net fees of SICAFs are subject to IRAP.	Exempt, taxation only on the taxable business.
Taxation at investors level	Withholding tax, no tax for pass-through entities.	Withholding tax, no tax for pass-through entities.

clear advantages if compared to the more recent alternatives represented by SIIQs and SICAFs.

Reserved real estate funds and SICAFs will continue to be the most profitable instruments for properties with upside potential, to be converted or valorised by active managers and marketed to investors with professional risk-management skills.

The strong and effective management quality and the well-defined role of each instrument will be of fundamental importance in terms of enhancement of asset value and increased profitability of real estate properties.

7 Performance of Italian closed-end AIFs

Issues in performance measurement

The legal framework of Italian real estate AIFs, i.e. real estate investment funds and SICAFs, has a relevant effect on their performance. The main factors of influence are their closed-end nature and the type of initial contribution (properties or capital).

Closed-end AIFs, given their finite time horizon, involve the presence of a management policy with a specific life cycle, including investment and divestment phases. During the investment phase, the AIF incurs in negative cash flows due to the acquisition, construction or renovation of properties, while, during the final divestment phase, the portfolio of real assets generates cash flows originating from the sales of properties. Between the two phases, the assets of the AIF are managed in order to compensate cash in- and outflows through the turnover of properties, facility and property management.

The performance measure coherent with this financial profile is the internal rate of return (IRR),[1] which can be calculated from two points of view: that of the manager of the AIF or of the investor in the AIF. In the former case, every cash flow of the AIF is included in the calculation, while in the latter case only the cash flows derived from subscription and the redemption of units/shares and from eventual profit distributions are relevant.

For these reasons, the IRR of a closed-end AIF can be determined only ex post. On the other hand, investors need periodical information before the maturity of the AIF, which can occur decades after the first capital contribution. As a consequence, it is necessary to calculate periodically the IRR, which becomes more accurate and representative of the ex post IRR the closer the AIF is to its maturity, T.

Borrowing from the experience of private equity industry, characterised by similar issues in performance measurement, two forms of IRR can be used.[2] The first one, i.e. the Gross Portfolio IRR (IRR_{GP}), measures the performance of investments made in a closed-end fund and is aimed at assessing the managers' ability to create value. The Gross Portfolio IRR, calculated at a time n (with $0 < n < T$), is the rate that sets the algebraic sum of the present values at the date of set up of the fund ($t = 0$) equal to zero:

- all cash outflows (OUT_t) paid by the fund into its portfolio of real assets;
- all cash inflows (IN_t) returned to the fund as rents, proceeds from the sale of properties, etc.;
- the properties and other assets at a specific date n (PP_n), assessed at fair value and net of liabilities.

The Gross Portfolio IRR is therefore the variable in the following equation, which can be estimated by an iterative process:

$$\sum_{t=0}^{n \leq T} \frac{OUT_t}{(1+IRR_{GP})^t} = \frac{PP_n}{(1+IRR_{GP})^T} + \sum_{t=0}^{n \leq T} \frac{IN_t}{(1+IRR_{GP})^t}$$

In the formula above, the date of sale of the properties is set at T as a conservative assumption. Moreover, the price of properties in T is unknown: as a result, it is considered to be identical to the value assessed when the Gross Portfolio IRR is calculated, i.e. at time, t.

The second formulation of the IRR is the Net Portfolio IRR (IRR_{NP}), measuring the return obtained by participants in a closed-end AIF by discounting all the cash outflows, i.e. the subscription units ($OUT_{part.,t}$), and inflows, such as the redemption of units and the distributions of income ($IN_{part.,t}$), taking into account also the NAV, which is assumed to be reimbursed at the maturity of the AIF.

The Net Portfolio IRR is therefore the variable in the following equation:

$$\sum_{t=0}^{n \leq T} \frac{OUT_{part.,t}}{(1+IRR_{NP})^t} = \frac{NAV_n}{(1+IRR_{NP})^T} + \sum_{t=0}^{n \leq T} \frac{IN_{part.,t}}{(1+IRR_{NP})^t}$$

Figure 7.1 shows the IRR of a real estate AIF with a maturity of 10 years. The IRR is recalculated every time that new information becomes available, i.e. the last cash flow or the last NAV. The last IRR shows the return up to that time and is calculated with increasing precision as the fund approaches its maturity.

The "J" shape of the IRR curve (J-curve) is known as the J-effect, a phenomenon which originates from the series of cash flows and from the different net value of the properties over time.[3] The J-curve can take on different shapes depending on the type of initial contribution to the AIF and to the asset allocation policy.

When the real assets are contributed to the AIF by its investors, usually the properties involved are already leased and therefore they generate

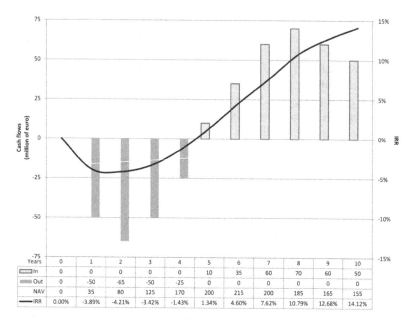

Years	0	1	2	3	4	5	6	7	8	9	10
In	0	0	0	0	0	10	35	60	70	60	50
Out	0	-50	-65	-50	-25	0	0	0	0	0	0
NAV	0	35	80	125	170	200	215	200	185	165	155
IRR	0.00%	-3.89%	-4.21%	-3.42%	-1.43%	1.34%	4.60%	7.62%	10.79%	12.68%	14.12%

Figure 7.1 The J-curve of the IRR.

Source: Adapted from Basile and Ferrari (2016).

positive cash flows deriving from rents. As a consequence, even though the contribution of real assets must be regarded as a figurative cash flow in order to calculate a correct IRR (both gross and net), the J-curve is usually less negative in the first years than in AIFs set up solely by capital contributions from their participants. In this case, in fact, the managers draw on the financial resources committed by investors only when they have identified the right investment opportunities.

The allocation policy regards, instead, the managers' strategies: they can focus on leased properties (core strategies), on the renovation of existing ones (value added strategies) or even on new developments (opportunistic strategies). More negative cash drawdown profiles are typical of opportunistic strategies, which therefore are characterised by sharper J-curves. Given the nature of Italian real estate AIFs, usually oriented to core strategies, the J-curve should not show a significant drawdown.

The IRR can be used to compare real estate AIFs, but it does not allow comparisons with financial assets belonging to different asset classes. For example, the returns of stocks are calculated on price changes and on the re-investment of dividends. On the other hand, the IRR is calculated on the trend over time and on the algebraic sum of a series of cash flows discounted at a conventional date.

In order to allow the comparison of such different performance measures it is possible to use the public market equivalent (PME). Various adaptations of this measure have been proposed over the years, due to the presence of distortions in its original formulation, but the most used is the Kaplan-Schoar PME.[4] The rationale of this indicator is to replicate the cash flows of the investment in real estate AIFs through a series of identical cash flows that focus on an equivalent portfolio, usually a stock market index. In other words, cash flows originating from investments in a real estate AIF are discounted at time zero, i.e. the date on which the AIF was set up, using the total returns of the equivalent portfolio as discount rates $(r_{0,t})$ from time zero to the time (t) of each cash flow. Finally, the PME is the ratio of the total discounted cash inflows, including the NAV at maturity T, to the total discounted outflows:[5]

$$PME = \frac{\dfrac{NAV_T}{1+r_{0,T}} + \sum_{t=0}^{T} \dfrac{IN_t}{1+r_{0,t}}}{\sum_{t=0}^{T} \dfrac{OUT_t}{1+r_{0,t}}}$$

The PME is above 1 if the IRR of the AIF is higher than the total return of the equivalent portfolio and under 1 in the opposite case.

From another point of view, the PME is the coefficient by which the cash flows invested in the equivalent portfolio must be multiplied in order to attain the same inflows that were generated by investing in the real estate AIF. For example, a PME of 1.7 implies that each outflow should be multiplied by 1.7 in order to reach the same result of the real estate AIF.

The PME method allows the calculation of the IRR of the equivalent portfolio. The sum of the outflows must be multiplied by the PME, using it as a scale factor. Then, instead of using the total returns of the equivalent portfolio as discount factors, the IRR is the variable in the following equation and is known as the PME IRR_{PME}:

$$PME \cdot \sum_{t=0}^{T} \frac{OUT_t}{(1+IRR_{PME})^t} = \frac{NAV_T}{(1+IRR_{PME})^T} + \sum_{t=0}^{T} \frac{IN_t}{(1+IRR_{PME})^t}$$

If the IRR_{PME} is higher than the IRR of the AIF, then the latter has attained a performance lower than the equivalent portfolio; vice versa, an IRR_{PME} lower than the IRR of the AIF indicates a better comparative performance. The IRR_{PME} spread, i.e. the difference between IRR and IRR_{PME}, measures the excess performance of the real estate AIF with respect to the equivalent portfolio.

Discount to NAV

When closed-end real estate AIFs are listed, they have two different capital gain profiles: variation in the NAV (ΔNAV) per unit or share and variation in market price. On the one hand, the ΔNAV per unit or share depends on the profit in the period (influenced not only by the returns of the real estate portfolio, but also by the level of debt) and the increase/decrease in the valuations of the real estate assets. On the other hand, the return for the investor prior to redemption on maturity is tied merely to the price movements of the units or shares in the investment vehicle traded in the market. Rarely these two returns match.

Market price and NAV are two quantities measured at distinct times. While the former may vary during every market session, the latter is published periodically in accordance with national regulations and the level of disclosure adopted. Outside the publication dates, the only variations in the published NAV known to investors regard the possible distribution of proceeds.[6] In order to take account of this asynchrony between the two values, the discount must not be calculated with reference to the published NAV, but to its value net of dividends paid, also known as adjusted NAV:

$$Adjusted\ NAV_T = NAV_{t=0} - \sum_{t=0}^{T} Dividends_t$$

The proceeds distributed in the period from $t = 0$ (publication date of the NAV) to T (date of calculation of the adjusted NAV) are subtracted from the NAV, as they constitute a reduction in the fund's net assets.[7] Therefore, the percentage discount of the market price compared to the NAV at time T equals:

$$Discount_T = \frac{Price_T - Adjusted\ NAV_T}{Adjusted\ NAV_T}$$

Market prices different from the NAV are not an isolated phenomenon typical only of real estate, but are part of the broader closed-end fund puzzle. While international literature on the theme is vast and has provided a list of the most relevant factors explaining discount to NAV in the real estate asset class,[8] here we will focus on the case of Italian real estate funds, given that no SICAFs have been listed yet.

Panetta (2009) has identified two main causal factors for NAV discount: liquidity on the secondary market and risk of the fund. The first factor is measured by the bid-ask spread and is inversely proportional to the discount, while the second is directly proportional and depends on financial leverage and the percentage of illiquid assets in the fund portfolio. Another, less relevant factor is the so-called "management quality," i.e. the ability of the fund manager to generate dividends higher than the management fees.

Morri and Benedetto (2009) have proposed an innovative technique, based upon the unlevered discount to NAV.[9] This analysis discards gearing as a driver of NAV discount, and instead points to other factors in order to explain this phenomenon. A lower discount is typical of funds that are predominantly held by institutional investors that invest a higher percentage of assets in properties, have been set up by contribution and, unexpectedly, are subject to higher management fees, probably because the quality of management is linked to its cost. On the contrary, NAV discount is lower for funds closer to maturity.

Biasin, Giacomini and Quaranta (2010) have focused their study on the governance of funds and its effect on the NAV discount, leading to the discovery that the presence of a unitholders' meeting decreases this negative phenomenon. Also the turnover of units on the secondary market, indicating a higher liquidity, causes a contraction in the discount, while the time to maturity is a factor positively related to discount to NAV.

Caporin, Lanzavecchia and Lippoli (2013) have underlined the mistrust of the market towards the appraisal value of properties held by real estate funds. A mistrust that, according to their analysis of 357 half-year reports, is not supported by empirical data, because funds usually sell their assets at prices higher than their appraisal value. Therefore, NAV discount seems to be excessive if compared to the fundamentals of the funds and therefore is based upon an irrational bias.[10]

Also Cacciamani and Ielasi (2006) have identified the lack of confidence of the market in expert valuers as a main driver in NAV discount, even though, according to their analysis, this market sentiment can be regarded as rational, due to the lack of transparency of the appraisals, typical of the sample object of analysis. This study has traced the causes of the discount to NAV also to other factors, such as the lack of geographic and sector diversification and the probability of extension of the fund maturity.

Empirical evidence

The prices of Italian listed real estate funds have suffered from the long economic crisis that has been taking place since 2008. As shown in Figure 7.2, the double-dip nature of this crisis is clearly represented by the BNP Paribas REIM Italian Real Estate Funds index.[11] Despite this downward trend, real estate funds have shown a performance less negative than the Italian stock market, represented by the FTSE MIB index. The correlation between these two indices has been of 0.46, highlighting the diversification potential of real estate in the Italian market.

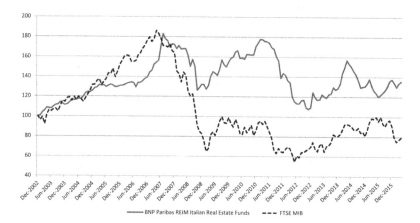

Figure 7.2 The performance of listed real estate funds and the stock market.
Source: Data from Morningstar Direct and BNP Paribas REIM.

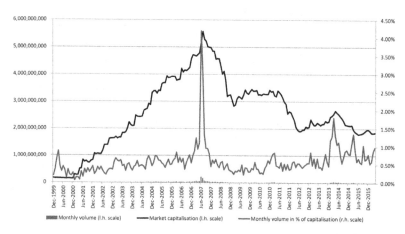

Figure 7.3 Capitalisation and volumes of Italian listed real estate funds.
Source: Borsa Italiana.

The BNP Paribas REIM IREF measures the monthly performance of real estate funds and is a capitalisation weighted total return index. Its calculation, therefore, takes into account the price return, dividends and other distributions:

$$\text{BNP Paribas REIM IREF} = \frac{price_t - price_{t-1} + dividend_{t-1} + reimbursement\ of\ units_{t-1}}{price_{t-1}}$$

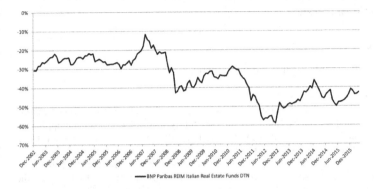

Figure 7.4 Discount to value of Italian real estate funds.

Source: Data from BNP Paribas REIM.

The market capitalisation of Italian real estate funds is about 1.9 billion euro, far from its apex of 5.5 billion euro in July 2007 (Figure 7.3). This is due not only to the contraction of prices, but also to the reimbursement of units as the funds have liquidated their properties.

Volumes are relatively thin, with a monthly turnover lower than 1% of total capitalisation, despite a positive trend in recent years.

Italian listed real estate funds are usually traded at a significant discount compared to the NAV. The relevance of this phenomenon, known as discount-to-NAV, is measured by the BNP Paribas REIM Italian Real Estate Funds DTN index, as shown in Figure 7.4.

The BNP Paribas REIM IREF DTN is capitalisation weighted and is calculated monthly, taking into account the adjusted NAV. The published NAV is included in calculations as soon as it is available. Moreover, given the delay of up to 2 months between the time of appraisal of the NAV and its announcement to the market, this index is "unfrozen," i.e. past values are recalculated when updated data are made public.

The mean discount to NAV has been equal to −34.56% since 2002, but with relevant differences in the past years. Until the summer of 2007 the discount was almost constant and with a lateral trend between −20% and −30%. The takeovers of some funds in mid 2007 have caused a contraction of NAV discount to its minimum of −11.67%. This short-lived phenomenon was followed by the first phase of the crisis, with a sudden surge in the NAV discount (−42.72% in October 2008). The apparent economic recovery of 2009–2011 came to a halt when the second phase of the double-dip crisis hit Italy, bringing the NAV discount to its maximum of −58.81% in November 2012. In recent years there has been a slow recovery, which had a strong acceleration in the summer of 2015 thanks to new takeover operations prompted by the initiative of British and US institutional investors.

Notes

1 Carretta, Fiordelisi and Mattarocci (2009).
2 IPEV (2012).
3 Baum (2015).
4 Kaplan and Schoar (2005), Harris, Jenkinson and Kaplan (2014). This measure, developed for the evaluation of private equity investments, has been applied to real estate closed end funds in recent studies, such as Fisher and Hartzell (2016).
5 Note that $1/(1 + r_{0,t})$ is the specific discount factor of each cash flow.
6 We use the expression "published NAV" to underline the fact that the daily changes in the NAV, as a result of the natural performance of the fund and the variation in the value of the real estate assets, are disregarded. This daily performance, in fact, is not calculated, in contrast to funds investing in listed assets, and therefore the only known NAV is that published periodically.
7 Working from an ex post point of view, we can estimate the NAV at time T by linear interpolation of the NAV at the beginning and end of the semester, as described in Biasin, Giacomini and Quaranta (2010).
8 Factors explaining discount to NAV are: leverage (Brounen and ter Laak, 2005), asset allocation (Capozza and Seguin, 1999), liquidity premium (Clayton and MacKinnon, 2001), potential recourse to grace period, and principal-agent costs (Capozza and Seguin, 2003).
9 The unlevered discount to NAV is calculated by adding the debt value to the NAV and to the market value both at the numerator and at the denominator.
10 Pattitoni, Petracci and Spisni (2013), analysing a smaller sample, have reached similar conclusions.
11 The number of components changed over time, from a minimum of 7 at its inception in December 2002 to a maximum of 25 in 2014. Since January 2015 the number of funds included in the calculation basket is 24.

References

Abate, G. (2011). Real Estate Finance e SGR immobiliari: Caratteristiche strutturali e dinamiche reddituali. *Bancaria*, 67(3), pp. 78–92.

ANCE (2015). *Osservatorio congiunturale sull'industria delle costruzioni*. Roma: ANCE.

Banca d'Italia (2015a). *Financial Stability Report*, 2015(2). Roma: Banca d'Italia.

Banca d'Italia (2015b). *Supplements to the Statistical Bulletin: Monetary and Financial Indicators. Financial Accounts*, XXV(54). Roma: Banca d'Italia.

Banca d'Italia (2016). *Financial Stability Report*, 2016(1). Roma: Banca d'Italia.

Basile, I. and Ferrari, P. (eds) (2016). *Asset Management and Institutional Investors*. Heidelberg: Springer.

Baum, A. (2015). *Real Estate Investment: A Strategic Approach*. 3rd edn. London: Routledge.

Biasin, M., Giacomini, E. and Quaranta, A. (2010). Public REITs' Governance and Regulatory Structure: Effects on NAV Discount. Evidence from the Italian Market. *Journal of European Real Estate Research*, 3(3), pp. 161–181.

Biasin, M. and Quaranta, A. (2012). Fondi immobiliari e commissioni di gestione ex GAV o NAV: Effetti sulla performance. *Banca, Impresa, Società*, 31(2), pp. 159–190.

Breuer, W. and Nadler, C. (eds) (2012). *Real Estate Finance*. Wiesbaden: Springer Gabler.

Brounen, D. and ter Laak, M. (2005) Understanding the Discount: Evidence from European Property Shares. *Journal of Real Estate Portfolio Management*, 11(3), pp. 241–251.

Cacciamani, C. and Ielasi, F. (2006). I fondi immobiliari retail quotati: andamento e prospettive. In: C. Giannotti, ed., *La gestione del fondo immobiliare: Rischio, diverisficazione e pianificazione*. Milano: Egea, pp. 61–90.

Caporin, M., Lanzavecchia, A. and Lippoli, V. (2013). I fondi immobiliari italiani: NAV discount e valutazione degli esperti indipendenti. *Finanza, Marketing e Produzione*, 31(3), pp. 147–171.

Capozza, D. and Seguin, P. (1999). Focus, Transparency and Value: The REITs Evidence. *Real Estate Economics*, 27(4), pp. 587–619.

Capozza, D. and Seguin, P. (2003). Inside Ownership, Risk Sharing and Tobin's q-Ratios: Evidence from REITs. *Real Estate Economics*, 31(3), pp. 367–404.

Carretta, A., Fiordelisi, F. and Mattarocci, G. (eds) (2009). *New Drivers of Performance in a Changing Financial World.* Basingstoke: Palgrave Macmillan.

Clayton, J. and MacKinnon, G. (2001). The Time-Varying Nature of the Link between REIT, Real Estate and Financial Asset Returns. *Journal of Real Estate Portfolio Management*, 7(1), pp. 43–54.

De Socio, A. (2010). La situazione economico-finanziaria delle imprese italiane nel confronto internazionale. *Banca d'Italia: Questioni di Economia e Finanza* (Occasional Papers), 66.

Fabrizi, C., Pico, R., Casolaro, L., Graziano, M., Manzoli, E., Soncin, S., Esposito, L., Saporito, G. and Sodano, T. (2015). Mercato immobiliare, imprese della filiera e credito: una valutazione degli effetti della lunga recessione. *Banca d'Italia: Questioni di Economia e Finanza* (Occasional Papers), 263.

Fisher, L. and Hartzell, D. (2016). Class Differences in Real Estate Private Equity Fund Performance. *Journal of Real Estate Financial Economics*, 52(4), pp. 327–346.

Gobbi, G. and Zollino, F. (2013). Le tendenze del mercato immobiliare e del credito, in Le tendenze del mercato immobiliare: l'Italia e il confronto internazionale. *Banca d'Italia: Workshops and Conferences*, 15.

Harris, R., Jenkinson, T. and Kaplan, S. (2014) Private Equity Performance: What Do We Know? *The Journal of Finance*, 69(5), pp. 1851–1882.

IPEV (2012). *International Private Equity and Venture Capital Investor Reporting Guidelines*, 1st edn. London: IPEV.

ISTAT (2015). *Le attività non finanziarie dei settori istituzionali: Anni 2005–2013.* Roma: ISTAT.

Just, T. and Maenning, W. (eds) (2012). *Understanding German Real Estate Markets.* Heidelberg: Springer.

Kaplan, S. and Schoar, A. (2005). Private Equity Performance: Returns, Persistence, and Capital Flows. *The Journal of Finance*, 60(4), pp. 1791–1823.

Morri, G. and Artegiani, A. (2015). The Effects of the Global Financial Crisis on the Capital Structure of EPRA/NAREIT Europe Index Companies. *Journal of European Real Estate Research*, 8(1), pp. 3–23.

Morri, G. and Benedetto, P. (2009). Leverage and NAV Discount: Evidence from Italian Real Estate Investment Funds. *Journal of European Real Estate Research*, 2(1), pp. 33–55.

Panetta, F. (ed.) (2009). L'andamento del mercato immobiliare italiano e i riflessi sul sistema finanziario. *Banca d'Italia: Questioni di Economia e Finanza* (Occasional Papers), 59.

Pattitoni, P., Petracci, B. and Spisni, M. (2013). NAV Discount in REITs: The Role of Expert Assessors. *Applied Economics Letters*, 20(2), pp. 194–198.

Sotelo, R. and McGreal, S. (eds) (2013). *Real Estate Investment Trusts in Europe: Evolution, Regulation, and Opportunities for Growth.* Heidelberg: Springer.

Index